Set Free
to Live Free

Set Free
to Live Free

Breaking Through the
7 Lies Women Tell Themselves

SAUNDRA DALTON-SMITH, MD

Revell

a division of Baker Publishing Group
Grand Rapids, Michigan

© 2011 by Saundra Dalton-Smith

Published by Revell
a division of Baker Publishing Group
P.O. Box 6287, Grand Rapids, MI 49516-6287
www.revellbooks.com

Printed in the United States of America

Library of Congress Cataloging-in-Publication Data

Dalton-Smith, Saundra, 1973–
    Set free to live free : breaking through the 7 lies women tell themselves / Saundra Dalton-Smith.
        p. cm.
    ISBN 978-0-8007-1993-7 (pbk.)
    1. Christian women—Religious life. 2. Self-talk—Religious aspects—Christianity. 3. Truthfulness and falsehood—Religious aspects—Christianity. 4. Self-actualization (Psychology)—Religious aspects—Christianity. I. Title.
BV4527.D28 2011
248.8′43—dc22   2010047548

Unless otherwise indicated, Scripture is taken from the *Holy Bible,* New Living Translation, copyright © 1996, 2004. Used by permission of Tyndale House Publishers, Inc., Wheaton, Illinois 60189. All rights reserved.

Scripture marked AMP is taken from the Amplified® Bible, Copyright © 1954, 1958, 1962, 1964, 1965, 1987 by The Lockman Foundation. Used by permission.

Scripture marked ASV is taken from the *American Standard Version* of the Bible.

Scripture marked CEV is taken from the Contemporary English Version © 1991, 1992, 1995 by American Bible Society. Used by permission.

Scripture marked KJV is taken from the King James Version of the Bible.

Scripture marked Message is taken from *The Message* by Eugene H. Peterson, copyright © 1993, 1994, 1995, 2000, 2001, 2002. Used by permission of NavPress Publishing Group. All rights reserved.

Scripture marked NCV is taken from the New Century Version®. Copyright © 1987, 1988, 1991 by Word Publishing, a division of Thomas Nelson, Inc. Used by permission. All rights reserved.

Scripture marked NIV is taken from the Holy Bible, New International Version®. NIV®. Copyright © 1973, 1978, 1984 by Biblica, Inc.™ Used by permission of Zondervan. All rights reserved worldwide. www.zondervan.com

Scripture marked NKJV is taken from the New King James Version. Copyright © 1982 by Thomas Nelson, Inc. Used by permission. All rights reserved.

11 12 13 14 15 16 17   7 6 5 4 3 2 1

To Fannie Mitchell and Emily Dalton,
you have both helped to heal the
pain of losing my mother at an early age.
It has been your faith that has shown me
the importance of believing and the healing power of love.

Contents

Acknowledgments 9

Part 1 Freedom Is a Choice

  1. Strange Medicine 13

  2. A Prescription for Living Free 21

Part 2 The Seven Lies Women Tell Themselves

    ▶ **Lie #1: Perfection**

  3. Perfection Is the Goal 36

  4. I Am Perfectly Imperfect 47

    ▶ **Lie #2: Envy**

  5. I Would Be Happy Too If I Had Her Life 58

  6. I Am Too Unique for Comparisons 68

    ▶ **Lie #3: Image**

  7. If I Do This, I Can Look Like That 79

  8. My Body, My Temple, God's Choice 91

Lie #4: Balance

9. Life Is an All-or-None Activity   105

10. My Balanced Life Requires Addition and Subtraction   116

Lie #5: Control

11. Being in Control Is Better Than Spontaneity   130

12. Spontaneity Is God's Opportunity to Surprise Me   142

Lie #6: Emotions

13. Emotional Imbalance Is Only for Crazy Women   154

14. My Transparency Opens the Door for Soul Connections   165

Lie #7: Limits

15. Everything Comes with Conditions   180

16. My Only Limitations Are the Ties I Allow to Bind Me   191

Part 3 The Free Woman's Creed

17. The Diamond Society   205

Eight-Week Group Study Guide   213

Acknowledgments

There are numerous people without whose support and assistance I could not have written this book. First, I would like to thank the many patients who allow me to be a part of their lives. I have taken the utmost care to preserve the confidential information with which you have entrusted me by altering the names and details of each case. Your triumphs are my motivation to see others free.

I am very grateful to my agent, Les Stobbe, for helping me dig deep to "write the book only you can write." You will never know how that one statement changed the whole way I look at writing.

A big thank you goes to Linda Nathan for editing the entire manuscript in an early draft. Your ability to retain the heart of the message while polishing grammar and flow is priceless.

My deepest appreciation to Baker Publishing Group for making this book a reality. A special thanks to Vicki Crumpton and Revell for shepherding this project to completion.

Last but hardly least, my heartfelt thanks go to my family. To my husband, Bobby, for his constant support and encouragement. And to our children, Tristan and Isaiah—your smiling faces, hugs, and affection make each day worth living to the fullest.

PART 1

Freedom Is a Choice

1

Strange Medicine

"Is this the last patient?" I asked my nurse, Shannon.

The lingering caffeine high of my morning coffee pushed me toward completing the morning roster of patients. I flipped through the notes for my patient in exam room seventeen. "What is her complaint?"

"She says she's here for a checkup, nothing more," Shannon offered as she collected charts from the finished bin.

I may be able to have lunch with my husband today, I thought as I walked through the door, unaware that the next few minutes would change how I practice medicine.

"I don't know why I'm here," Cameron sputtered, her words racing out in one breath. "I thought maybe there would be something that could help me. I should probably leave before I waste any more of your time."

Cameron's thirty-eight-year-old frame was ample but carried a heaviness that had nothing to do with physical weight. This was her third office visit with me. The first two were basic visits detailing her general health issues. High blood pressure, headaches, and weight were her main areas of concern. Nothing about her prior visits prepared me for this one. The atmosphere around today's visit had a tangible charge that threatened to ignite at any moment.

"Why don't you tell me what's going on. Who knows— maybe I will be able to help. You'll never know unless you give me a chance." I smiled patiently.

"I think I'm depressed," Cameron confessed. "I just don't find any happiness in my life anymore. It seems that everyone else is enjoying their life while I just exist day-to-day."

"I understand," I said with empathy.

"How could you possibly understand?" she spat out with a shudder in her voice. A single tear betrayed the personal boundaries she attempted to maintain. "You've got it all! How can you possibly understand what it feels like to go to bed beside a man who doesn't find you physically attractive? How could you know what it's like to feel like an outsider, like you are not good enough? When I pick up my kids at school all the other women look at me like I'm worthless, like I'm not even visible."

Self-pity moved into open anger as her voice rose with each word. "I just don't see the point of even trying. Nothing I do is ever good enough. I try to be like those other women. I really do want to lose weight, but it's just not easy for me. I don't know what I am doing wrong. Why can't I be happy and have friends like everyone else? Why does my life have to be so hard?"

By now Cameron had relinquished all pretense of control, and the tears flowed freely down her face. Years of frustration washed out of her psyche, if only for those few brief moments of transparency. The intimacy of the emotions on display was in direct contrast to the coldness of the small medical exam room. I placed my hand on Cameron's shoulder in an attempt to comfort her. But before I could speak she shrugged off my gesture and said, "I don't need your pity."

Cameron's eyes never left the ground. I realized that throughout our whole interaction she had not looked directly at me, not even once. She sat with her hands in her lap, silent. Not a glance in my direction. Fortunately, Cameron was my last patient for that morning and had happened into my life at a time when I actually could help her, but not in the way she expected.

"No, you don't need my pity; you are doing a good job pitying yourself," I said with a calmness that surprised even me. I didn't say it to be spiteful but just as a matter of fact.

My statement caught Cameron off guard. Her eyes were like large brown marbles, glossy from the pain they echoed. Obviously I had hit a soft spot, and in her fragile state she was not able to contain herself. It was as if in one sharp blow I cut through the fragments that held her together. The sobs that left her body caused her entire being to shake from the force.

I don't know if we stayed in that position for five seconds or five minutes, but it felt like hours. Silently I watched the young mother and wife digest the strange medicine I was administering. *Please, God, help her receive this the right way*, I silently prayed.

As the sobs quieted down to sniffles, I handed her a box of tissues and for the first time Cameron looked directly at me. "I don't know what's wrong with me. I'm never like this. I'm not some emotional crazy woman. It's just been a hard few months."

⟨◈⟩

Cameron and her family had lived in the area for ten months. She and Roger had two children, Rachel who had just turned five and Jacob who was three. Five years ago Cameron quit her job to become a stay-at-home mom. She loved her kids and had not regretted for one second her decision to be available to them around the clock. But with Rachel starting kindergarten and Jacob going to preschool, Cameron knew she needed to transition into the next phase of her life.

Cameron was excited that she had done such a great job raising confident and happy kids. She was ready to find a part-time job while the kids were at school. She had felt certain she wouldn't have any problem landing a job with her excellent work history, but five resumes had not elicited a single callback. *They must have misplaced my applications,* she thought. However, calling one of the agencies confirmed her worst fears.

The man on the other end of the line stated in a clipped voice, "I'm sorry, but you've been out of the business for over five years, and we need someone with current experience." As she placed the phone back on the hook, a wave of nausea overtook her. She sat with her head resting on the toilet seat, a feeling of defeat washing over her.

The next morning she headed to the school library where she volunteered a few days a week in an attempt to meet new friends. But the other moms treated her as if she were the help and not an equal. It was as if they were able to look directly past her. No hellos, no invitations to coffee or lunch. Today was her second month volunteering, and she was determined to meet someone.

As a group of volunteer moms set off to reshelf books, Cameron approached one young mother with a daughter in Rachel's class. "Hi, I'm Cameron," she muttered.

"Oh, hi," responded the young woman with a giggle. "Is this your first day volunteering in the library? Why do you think they put some books up so high? How could a child ever reach them?" And with that she marched off to regroup with her friends, waving as she said, "Bye Carol, it was nice meeting you." Despite the fact that the young woman had forgotten her name, Cameron was more disturbed that the woman hadn't even told her *her* name. *Am I that insignificant?* she thought.

Roger returned home that night to find the house disheveled and Cameron munching on chips with the kids. His glib statement about the dirty dishes in the sink was not meant as a personal attack, but that's how Cameron saw it. Dinner was a silent exchange as Cameron mentally pored over all that had gone wrong. That evening Roger fled into the living room to watch television.

Cameron put the kids to bed and began her nightly routine. Her glance fell upon her reflection in the mirror. Where had those lines come from between her eyes? When did her hips begin to spread like her mother's? Why was it that everyone else seemed able to bounce back to their prepregnancy bodies but she had to deal with her C-section bulge? Life just didn't seem fair. She did her best to freshen up. She knew it had been over a week since she and Roger had been intimate. *At least he still loves me*, she thought. She slipped on the chemise he always complimented her on, followed by a splash of perfume.

Roger knew something was wrong, but he didn't know how to deal with it. He spotted Cameron as she approached the bed. He always loved it when she wore that chemise but knew tonight wasn't the time to try to approach her. *Cameron is definitely not in the mood for sex*, he thought. So instead of starting another fight, he opted to keep silent and merely said, "Good night, love."

Loved is exactly what Cameron did not feel. Not from Roger, not from God, and not even from herself. As she closed her eyes, she thought about cancelling her doctor's appointment for the following morning. *What's the use?* she thought. *Oh well, if nothing else maybe she can give me something to help make me feel better.*

"What exactly is it that's causing you so much distress?" I interjected. "What area of your life do you feel is weighing you down?"

"That's just it," Cameron began. "I have no idea what my problem is, but life just does not seem to work out for me. It's not just one area; it's every aspect of my life. I had so many plans and dreams growing up. The older I get, the further away I get from making those dreams a reality. It seems that no matter how hard I try, I just can't make my plans happen the way I envision them."

Cameron was absentmindedly twirling a curly strand of hair around her finger as she stared at a landscape scene on the opposite wall. The tears had ceased, replaced by a solemn resolve that her fate was sealed. Life was not fair and she would always end up on the short side of the deal.

This young woman sitting across from me was in some ways a mirror reflection of my own personal life. We both were married with young kids. We were both in our late thirties. The main difference was our view about our lives. Cameron had incorporated a wrong set of personal beliefs into the tapestry of her life. This faulty belief system was choking the joy out of her, mentally keeping her from being open to experiencing and enjoying the unique elements of her life.

Like bacteria, these mental lies had gained access through an open wound in her life. Initially they may only have affected one aspect of her life, but daily they grew stronger until ultimately they had begun to weave themselves around vital areas. Her health, joy, and self-confidence, as well as her ability to love and be loved, could now feel the tightening grip of these mental ties. Before she realized what was happening, they had started draining the life out of her life.

"Cameron, do you want to get better, or have you completely given up hope of being happy?" I asked as compassionately as I could for such an in-your-face question. I knew there was a fifty percent chance she'd grab her bag and leave the office, but there was an equal chance she would give me the opportunity to help her.

Cameron sat motionless for over a minute. When the emotions of the past weeks subsided, she honestly contemplated the question. "I do want to be better," she said as her lips slanted up in the faintest of smiles. "I haven't completely given up hope yet, but I don't know how much more I can take."

I beamed. "Good. I don't have a magic pill that's going to make everything better overnight. What I am offering you is an opportunity to heal an area of your mind that has been wounded and bound."

Cameron's face yielded to a look of confusion. "What are you talking about?"

"I'm talking about freeing your mind from the lies that have caused you to see life from a disadvantaged perspective. These lies have become a mental tie, limiting your ability to enjoy your life. You're right, you are not crazy. Nor do I believe that at this time you need a medication, or at least not in the sense you were expecting. What I am prescribing for you are five stages of freedom. Navigating each stage brings you one step closer to being completely free in your spirit."

"I don't understand," whispered Cameron as she shook her head in disbelief over my proposal.

"What I am proposing to you is a chance to actively work through the areas of your life that are causing you so much distress. Your only limitations are the ties you allow to bind you. If you don't break this cycle, it will continue to control you."

"Do you want to be free?" I probed for the final time.

"I do."

"Then let's begin . . ."

2

A Prescription for Living Free

I glanced at the clock on the far wall: noon. Thirty minutes had passed from the time I entered Cameron's room, but really our visit was only now beginning.

Hands clamped in her lap, Cameron did not say a word, but her body language spoke volumes. She might as well have been handcuffed. She was shackled, held back from reaching out for the very things she needed to find peace and happiness. Cameron had no idea when she became bound, but she could feel the suffocating effects. She was anxious for release and willing to try whatever help I could offer.

I had never prescribed such an unusual therapy to a patient. Medical training had ill prepared me for the spiritual and psychological counseling needed to help Cameron. Life experience and personal revelation merged with my board-certified internal medicine knowledge. Had she arrived at my door eight years ago, I would not have been able to help her. I could have given Cameron any number of antidepressants, but such an approach would only have been a Band-Aid on a wounded life. What

Cameron needed was freedom from the messages she had allowed to permeate her spirit. The same mental ties had once bound me: comparisons, perfectionism, calloused emotions, body envy, and a controlling mentality, just to name a few.

It took many years of wandering around an emotional desert to reach a place of day-by-day, step-by-step working through the lies that limited me. I have the privilege of intimate access into the lives of women from various age groups, educational levels, and socioeconomic conditions. Daily I glean information from the lives of these women who successfully overcame life's challenges. I nicknamed this sisterhood of overcomers the Diamond Society. My findings helped me to overcome my own personal struggles, and now it was time to share what I had learned.

One key component these overcomers had in common was a grounded belief and trust in Jesus. They were certain not only that he existed, but that he was able to do more in their lives than they could possibly ask or think. He was not a religious figure but a daily acquaintance, a confidant, a beloved friend. To them he was not someone to be talked about, but rather someone to talk to. While some women found their way to a psychotherapist's couch for consultation, this sisterhood found themselves on their living room couches confiding in the Great Counselor.

Religion has no place in a doctor's office, or at least that is what society would suggest. The reality is that when people are the sickest, God is often in the forefront of their minds: "Does he exist? Does he care about me and my personal situations? Can I be made whole again?" What better time to confront an issue than when it has pushed itself to the center stage of your life.

"Cameron, do you believe in God?" I asked with much hesitation, almost to the point of stuttering. Evangelism is something I never believed I would be able to do, and I had not planned to start today. But if I learned anything from the Diamond Society, I knew that without a solid faith foundation, no amount of help would get Cameron to her goals.

"Of course I believe there is a God. I just don't know about all the weird stuff. You know, all this Jesus stuff. I mean, if he walked on water and raised dead people. I went to church when I was young, but it all just seems so impossible."

Cameron's gaze seemed focused on a point outside of the room. It was an unusual stare, as if she were peeking into a scene beyond our current reality, looking down a past road of hurt or pain, back at a moment of time that held her fixated. It was the same stare I'd seen once before in the eyes of my youngest child, Isaiah.

I recalled being at a large gathering with him and my oldest son, Tristan. Isaiah was always a rambunctious, adventurous child, so when I took my eyes off him for a few seconds to help his brother he wandered off. I remember turning around to find him no longer at my side. I frantically looked around but could not easily see him in the crowd. Kneeling down to finish tying Tristan's shoes so we could go find him, I spotted a small figure crouched in the corner. The look in Isaiah's eyes matched Cameron's. He was not crying but rather was fixated in his place of perceived abandonment. When he spotted me, a smile of recognition caused his face to crumble into an avalanche of bewildered tears. He climbed into my arms and clung to me as if his life depended on it.

Abandonment has a way of making you retreat into a place that blocks out emotions. Whether it's actual or perceived abandonment makes no difference to the one feeling the pain. The solution: a reunion with the one you believe left you.

"When did he leave?" I asked softly, unsure where the conversation would lead.

Cameron cleared her throat as if doing so helped to clear her mind. "Excuse me, when did who leave?"

"Jesus," I answered. "When did he let you down? When did he abandon you in your time of need?"

Cameron did not answer with words. With one hand she covered a small locket she wore around her neck and clung to it for dear life. The wrinkle in her brow and its arch of pain seemed to contour her entire face, echoing a deep wound. I don't know what was in that locket; to this day, Cameron has not shared whatever painful memory it held. Whether it was a child or a parent that met an untimely death, I will never know.

"Cameron, I don't know why bad things happen," I continued. "But I do know that there is a God and he has a son named Jesus. I am convinced that they both love you very much. Whatever pain is contained in your locket was never sent to destroy you. Jesus has not abandoned you, nor has he ever left your side. If you will look for him, you will find that he has been present all along. It's time to release the pain and cling to him."

We didn't say the sinner's prayer. We didn't read a Bible verse. If I were being graded at a seminary, I would have failed miserably on the evangelism test. But I believe there is power in the name of Jesus and that just saying it out loud has the ability to change the chemistry of the soul.

Cameron didn't say anything for a long time. As we concluded her office visit, the heavy sensation that had permeated the room had lifted. Her hunched shoulders had smoothed out into anatomically correct slopes. She left with clarity in her eyes that had not been present, a tangible change in her personal aura. The possibility of hope was in the air. We scheduled weekly visits at eleven thirty, the same time slot as our initial visit. On a prescription pad I scribbled five words in my best messy-doctor-penmanship: illumination, activation, transition, expulsion, detachment. I asked Cameron to define each word prior to her next visit and to meditate on the potential each has in its ability to change her life.

The Five Stages of Freedom

Stage 1: Illumination—Peek Inside Yourself

Light can be an ally or a nemesis. Sitting at a vanity with palettes of eye shadow, blush, foundation, and lip liner, a woman has all the tools for a successful makeover. Use the wrong light, however, and you can easily end up looking like a clown. One well-placed fluorescent light can illuminate the intrinsic hues in the makeup and, more importantly, in your skin tone. The right light helps you see the true you. Every blemish and imperfection is laid bare beside every area of smooth complexion. After taking an inventory of what you have to work with, the artist in you can visualize what you want the canvas to display and work toward that goal.

Life is a canvas on which to create and dream. Each person is designed to be a unique work of art breathed into being by the Master Creator. However, each person has the same purpose: to bring glory and praise to the Creator. Art should not be hidden but displayed for others to experience and enjoy. Have you noticed that fine art is typically placed under a spotlight? How better to see the fine details stroked into existence behind the central scene? What better way to see the signature of the artist on the work, signifying his approval of the finished product? You are a work in progress that God wants to illuminate.

Crafted into the details of your personal story are unique colors of life. The pastels of joy and peace, the neutral colors of everyday activities, the vivid streaks of past pains and trials, and the bold accents of triumph and victory. Without these variations, each life would become a carbon copy of the one before it. Thankfully, the Master Creator is not out of ideas on how to create unique masterpieces out of the ups and downs of our lives—masterpieces that once on display have the potential to convey a message to all who see them.

As living art forms, we have the ability to move in and out of the light. We can choose whether to be illuminated for deeper examination by ourselves and others. Or we can choose to remain in the shadows where we will only see in part who we were designed to be, limiting our ability to inspire. You are the number one observer of your life's art, and you deserve an illuminated view. If you look closely enough you will see the Master Creator's signature of approval written upon you.

Stage 2: Activation—Change Is Hard Work and It May Involve Sweat

Living requires energy. Every aspect of daily life requires a certain degree of energy transfer from your physical and mental reserves. The law of energy states that energy cannot be created or destroyed but only transferred. This law is true physically and spiritually. Like a rechargeable battery, each night you have the opportunity to physically plug in for seven hours of rejuvenation. From the time you wake until you return for another fill-up, you will transfer your newly gained energy into various activities such as carpooling, working, and laundry.

It is just as important to recharge spiritually. Maintaining relationships, supporting family, and uplifting friends can zap all of last Sunday's worship high right out of you. Leave your spiritual battery off the hook for too long and watch how quickly you begin to see the flashing red warning signs of eventual shutdown. Depression, anxiety, fear, emotional eating, ambivalence, anger, impatience, insomnia, muscle tension, and fatigue are all indicators of a depleted energy source.

The emotional ties with the past that we need to cut can be painful, causing us to resist the discomfort of change and remain in familiar areas. As long as your life proceeds down a course of least resistance, you require only a minimum amount of energy due to the forward momentum of your set course. To change the course you must overcome the momentum, the barriers that block your source of positive energy.

Mental ties are barriers separating your life into two pools of energy. On one side is a negative pool of energy that can cause you to see yourself as a runner-up in life. On the other side is a positive pool of energy that can reaffirm your soul with a refreshing bath of confidence. How do you overcome the barrier to get from the negative pool to the positive? Activation energy.

Activation energy is the energy that you need for a change to occur. It is the push that causes you to gravitate toward a new way of thinking, a new way of living. Activation energy moves you toward the promises of God. It propels you like an arrow toward the bull's-eye of God's best for your life. It sets in motion a series of events that has the potential to transfer positive, life-giving energy back into the dying areas of your life.

Stage 3: Transition—Stretched to the Max but Rebounding with Grace

Change is not easy, but with the right momentum it can become easier. When you jump on a trampoline, gravity will pull the weight of your body downward along the course of least resistance. The gravity of past pain, unrealistic expectations, and self-defeatism can just as easily pull you down a path of unhappiness.

Once your weight hits the barrier (the trampoline), you have a choice to make. If you fall passively on the trampoline, each bounce will take you lower and lower until your momentum stops. But if you put energy back into the trampoline by jumping, you will rebound higher and higher.

Feeling stretched to the max? Which will it be, crash or rebound? Now is the time to decide to transition to a higher level of thinking. You may feel you are at the breaking point, but use that energy to rebound with grace. Bounce right out of that mental fog into a place of clarity, a place without limitations based on societal norms but covered by the grace to live free.

The transition state is like a pit. It is the place where a decision must be made. After illumination you will either gain the activation energy to climb out of your mental pit or you will remain in your current position. If mental ties have kept you in a holding pattern, now is the time to reassess. Can you sense the winds of change propelling you toward freedom? Conquering the transition state is vital in successfully overcoming the lies you have been telling yourself. It is the pivotal stage and the one in which the greatest resistance will occur. It will involve stretching, but there is grace to rebound. Now is the time to learn the rhythm of grace.

Stage 4: Expulsion—Dynamic Interference Required

External life forces can move you. There are pleasant forces that can move you in a positive direction and negative forces that can hinder you. From the warm bear hug of a five-year-old to the coffee that spills on your blouse just before an important meeting, external events produce a dynamic flow of feelings within you. External forces can be as benign as the examples above or as toxic as size 0 models who make us hate our own bodies. The dynamics of the external force depend on how long it is applied. The longer you are exposed to the force, the more it can move you. All dynamic forces have the ability to produce movement in how you respond and how you feel, unless interference is interjected.

What is interference? Interference blocks your ability to receive a clear signal from the external source. It halts the ongoing momentum produced by the force. It's like a mental gatekeeper that deciphers whether something is worth holding onto or if it should be expelled. The deciding factor is, how does it move you? Does it move you toward a happy, fulfilled life, or does it cause condemnation, guilt, or shame?

Whatever controls the focus of your mind controls your life. Mental ties produce movement toward self-condemnation, and such thoughts must be forcefully expelled for freedom to arise. You must experience a "suddenly" moment where enough is enough and you explosively reject all aspects of those lies. The expulsion stage ejects the deep-rooted mind-set from your modus operandi. No longer is it an acceptable way of thinking, but it is vigorously replaced with a new mode of operation, a mode that allows you to embrace individuality, spontaneity, affirmation, and freedom.

Each time a web of that mental tie tries to entangle itself around your life, positive interference can interrupt to break the bond. Scripture, worship, prayer, and positive affirmations are all forms of interference that can break the restricting power of these lies. There is life and death in the power of the tongue. You become what you believe. What you say about yourself to yourself matters, so it's important that you say positive things. Expulsion causes your internal worth to rise up like an artesian well with a deep reserve to declare what God says about who you are and what you can do.

Stage 5: Detachment—Cut the Ties (Snip, Snip)

Some things are meant to be lost. What mental baggage have you collected along your life journey? You can overcome past attachments to negative concepts and mind-sets. As God's plan of freedom opens to you, it weakens the status of negative mental ties. Each spiritual promise snips away at binding thoughts and allows movement toward a happier life. All thoughts of limitation, inferiority, or insignificance become permanently cut out of your life, a final detachment that releases you to be confidently and uniquely content to be you. •

Putting your life under a microscope may not sound like a fun weekend activity, but it became the basis for a series of life sessions that allowed Cameron to release old fatal concepts about herself and to embrace the mind of a free woman. Over the course of a few months, we systematically worked through seven lies she believed about herself. Cameron became the first of numerous women who have discovered that some of the best prescription medications do not come in bottles but rather in the form of a journal, a quiet space, and raw emotions. You cannot destroy what you will not confront. Blunted emotions, lack of joy, lack of energy, fear, and anxiety are all by-products of mental ties, but you can be free to enjoy your life.

<hr />

In part 2 we will discuss seven different women battling specific lies, or as I like to refer to them, mental ties. Some of these lies are perpetuated daily in the media, culture reiterates some, and some are pressures within certain socioeconomic groups. The women are wives, moms, and daughters just like you, who by no fault of their own have been drained of a free spirit. No matter how easily a mental tie may have wormed itself into your mind, it is time to stop any further progression and move toward living freely. We will work through all five stages of each lie. Each section will have a chapter describing one of the lies, followed by a chapter describing a new free mind-set. Soon you too will be able to live the Free Woman's Creed, seven statements of freedom that will release you into a life of confident assurance of God's goodness.

PART 2

The Seven Lies
Women Tell Themselves

Perfection

3

Perfection Is the Goal

"Has anyone else ever felt like choking some of the women in the Bible, or is it just me?" Rebecca questioned.

"I don't know about you, but occasionally I have an overwhelming desire to pencil in a few extra verses to Proverbs 31, like: 'She sitteth on the couch and watcheth Oprah,' or 'She eateth ice cream right out of the carton.' Then there is Deborah with her overwhelming courage. Esther with her exquisite beauty and grace. Let's not forget Mary, the matriarch of faith, who without a word of worry or protest believed God one hundred percent and birthed the impossible. Each of these ladies is a great woman of faith, but they are very high measuring rods by which to gauge myself. Personally, none are a reflection of me; I am a habitual screwup. So remind me again why we spend so much time studying these women?"

Rebecca was new to this particular Bible study group, but she was in no way new to church. As a preacher's daughter she was well versed in the Bible. Religion was a way of life for Rebecca. Church services, Bible studies, prayer sessions, conferences—you name it and Rebecca had likely attended. However, today Rebecca was not in the mood for more religion. Sitting quietly listening to another story about how great these women were only made her feel worse about her seemingly constant personal failures.

Looking over the past year of newlywed life, Rebecca was even more convinced that she was not a good wife or future mother material. There were no Rachael Ray–style meals served at her home for dinner. Boxed macaroni and cheese with frozen chicken nuggets were her standard culinary delights. No one was going to give her the Martha Stewart award for best decorated home. For that matter, Martha would be banned from her home for fear of what she would say about the stack of dirty dishes in the sink and the Coke stains on the carpet. Rebecca couldn't stay on a diet and exercise program faithfully for more than a few weeks, so she certainly didn't want the responsibility of sole nutritional provider during nine months of pregnancy. What if something was wrong with the baby? Wouldn't she be the one at fault for her lack of consistent vitamin consumption or for not keeping her stress under control?

Rebecca did not see the point in finding yet one more woman with whom to compare herself. So when the topic of the new Bible study group was announced—Great Women of Faith—Rebecca met her breaking point. The poised twenty-eight-year-old needed to know if she was the only one ready to snatch out those sections of the Bible that seemed to taunt her existence. Little did Rebecca know, her outburst was the window into her soul through which others could find a point of entry to help her. At the conclusion of the Bible study, one of the ladies recommended that Rebecca come see me for a checkup.

"She's not your typical doc," Cameron said with a smile. "Believe me when I say to expect the unexpected."

Cameron was weeks into her own counseling sessions and well on her way to freedom. Having already worked through the first mental tie, Cameron could easily spot the signs of bondage in others.

Lie #1: Perfection Is the Goal

Someone once said, "When you aim for perfection, you discover it's a moving target." Unfortunately many women have not attained this revelation. Rather than changing their goal, they try in vain to hit the impossible. Every day women mentally berate themselves for not completing their to-do list: feeling guilty over not having enough time to cook meals for their families; increased anxieties over the unfinished loads of laundry and dishes; condemnation over every morsel of food with over 30 percent fat; fears that their parenting will in some way miss the mark and result in irreparable damage to their children's future; irrational expectations that following the latest diet program will give them the gorgeous body on the magazine cover. Their increasing disappointment in their failed attempts only results in a rise in negative self-talk and a decline of self-esteem.

My fondest memories as a little girl are the times I spent daydreaming about what life would be like as an adult. I can recall the hours spent thinking through every detail. From the height of my husband to the eye color of my children, I painted a perfect mental picture of how my happy life would look. During my teen years the details became more elaborate as I added in college and career plans. Then as time passed it became increasingly obvious that things were not going to happen as easily as they did in my daydreams. When I became a wife and mother, I found myself continually tweaking my current life to fit my idea of perfection. Apparently God did not get the memo about my perfect life requirements.

Where does this lie come from? How is it so deeply rooted in our beliefs? "Practice makes perfect." "You are a picture of perfection." "She has the perfect life." These are just a few of the statements that perpetuate the myth that perfection exists on this side of heaven. From early childhood, we all love the books with happy endings where everything falls into place without a hitch. The process builds through the impressionable tween and teen years as we absorb what we see on television and in movies and magazines. Each image adds interlocking links to our picture of the life we desire to live one day. Each link reinforces the bond, making it even harder to freely experience the ebb and flow of life without feeling strained and stressed.

"Perfect" and "normal" are both products of the same mutant gene pool and do not exist in the general population. I have learned that perfection only occurs in print and media. It is a vapor of life that the media vainly tries to capture and preserve lest it quickly slip away. The actors whose lives look so perfect on screen are just that—actors playing a part. Someone tells them how they should feel, what they should say, and how they should respond within the confines of their characters. Who wants to live a confined, pre-scripted life?

Unfortunately, many of us women have written scripts for our own lives in our minds, daily striving to live out the "perfect" life. Those scripts are based on our own preconceived expectations of what we feel is required to be successful, fulfilled, and happy. When our striving fails to produce the results we want, we feel confused because life hasn't followed our scripts. These times of missing the mark lead to disappointment and test our faith—not just our faith in God, but also our faith in our own ability to script our perfect lives.

When you live your life as the lead character in "My Perfect Life," you set yourself up for frustration because you lose the real you within the role you are portraying. You lose your ability to accept your God-given individuality, preferences, strengths, and weaknesses. You lose your ability to accept your imperfections as a part of your uniqueness. Once you accept the fact that you are not perfect and will never be perfect, you can then develop the confidence to embrace freedom.

Freedom can be scary when you've become locked into bonds. Each new bend in life pulls and stretches you to be open to the possibility of happiness outside of your pre-planned course. Can you be happy if you never reach your ideal body weight? Can peace replace guilt when you opt for takeout rather than cooking at home? Can expectation replace anxiety when there is an interruption in your daily schedule?

Living free is not synonymous with settling for less. It doesn't mean you should not dream. It is not an excuse to lose your vision or your desires for your future. What it does mean is being open to the possibility that God may have an even better plan than the one you scripted. When you spend your days holding out for everything to be perfect, you may end up with nothing.

Illumination—*Peek Inside Yourself*

Wanting to improve is not a bad quality. We should all desire to improve our lives. However, when the basis of that desire is a false perception that by improving you will be able to reach some level of perfection, the scale tips toward absolute failure. None of us will always get it right in life. We will make wrong decisions. Mistakes will occur. Throughout the process it is vital to maintain the ability to forgive yourself for your shortcomings.

Do any of the following statements describe you?

- If I make a bad decision, I criticize myself for a long time afterward.
- I have trouble forgiving myself when I make a decision that turns out to be poor.
- I feel that if I make a mistake in my parenting, my children will be irreversibly damaged.
- I am constantly reading how-to books on ways to improve myself.
- No matter how hard I try, I can never be as good a wife or mother as I would like to be.
- I want everyone to like me.
- I can be very critical of others when I feel they don't hold themselves up to the same high standards that I have for myself.
- I feel guilty because I believe I can never do enough for my family.
- My kids say I criticize them too much.
- I get upset with myself if I don't get the top positions within my career field.
- When I look at a project I have done, all I can see are the imperfections.
- My fear of doing something poorly sometimes prevents me from getting started.
- I cannot go to bed until the house is clean and the dishes are washed.
- I get upset with myself when I am cooking something and it does not turn out like the picture in the cookbook.
- I feel that my home will never be as nicely decorated, organized, or clean as I would like it to be.
- I feel disappointed with my body when I get sick.

- If I eat anything that I feel is not healthy, I feel guilty and mad at myself.

These statements can be rooted in a prideful mentality that says we are too perfect for such mishaps to occur in our lives. ("How dare that dish fail to come out picture-perfect?") Or they can be rooted in a fatalistic mentality that our imperfections disqualify us from lives of happiness. ("I can't cook like my mom, so why bother.") While the approach in each case is different, the underlying lie remains the same: perfection is the goal.

Activation—*Change Is Hard Work and It May Involve Sweat*

The most common feelings associated with perfectionist thoughts are disappointment, guilt, anger, fear, and shame, which produce a flow of negative energy. Rebecca had progressed through the illumination stage on her own and arrived at my office ready to use her negative emotions as the activation energy needed to propel her toward a positive life change.

Her years of living under the pretense of perfection had caused quite a buzz when the reality was unleashed at that Wednesday afternoon women's Bible study. Although I was not present, word of her outburst had spread like wildfire, reaching all the way to my third-row pew seat. So when Rebecca's name appeared on my patient list the following week, I was not surprised.

"Well, Rebecca, that must have been some Bible study discussion." I smiled as I walked into the room.

Her nervous giggle showed that she still felt self-conscious about her outburst. "It was definitely one to remember. I love God, and I do think all those women we were discussing are phenomenal. I don't know," she admitted, "it just seemed so overwhelming on that day."

"What about that day was different from every other day?" I probed. "I mean, I'm sure you've had these feelings before, so what made you respond so strongly on that particular day?"

Rebecca sat pensively for a few moments. Then, as if a light switch had flipped on, she sat upright in her chair. "I hadn't associated these two events, but now I'm certain that they're related," she continued. "Earlier that week I had my mother and father over for dinner. I was so stressed out about having them over to the house. Since the wedding, we've only visited at their house, not at mine. My mother likes for everything to be immaculate. I did my best to make sure my house would pass her standard and failed miserably. She had suggestions on how I could accessorize to bring out the colors in one room, or how I could enrich the flavors of my pot roast. Everything was wrong in her eyes. I entered an emotional slump after that dinner that stayed with me for days.

"I thought I'd gotten over it, but apparently I hadn't. So when the women's Bible study group started talking about more women I'd never be able to measure up to, it seemed like a personal attack on me." Rebecca's face shone with enlightenment.

"Who do you believe initiated this personal attack?" I asked.

"I assume my mother started it," she stated matter-of-factly.

"Your mother may have given you some additional ammunition," I agreed. "But actually the personal attack began long before she arrived at your home. It started in your own mind."

As Rebecca mulled over my statement, I continued. "The personal attack started the moment you began fretting over your home, your housekeeping skills, and your cooking. I am sure you're familiar with the spiritual law that states we reap what we sow. You sowed a negative energy in the atmosphere of your home that reaped more negative energy. Your mother simply participated within the atmosphere created."

Rebecca nodded in understanding. Having a fundamental knowledge of the biblical law of sowing and reaping had failed to open her mind to the possibility that the law works even in the mundane areas of life.

"Why did you feel that your best would not be enough?" I questioned.

"I just wanted to show my parents that things were going well with the marriage and that I could take care of myself. I wanted them to have a good first impression of our home. I wanted them to be proud of me."

"There's nothing wrong with wanting to show your independence, nor is there anything wrong with wanting to make your parents proud. Having known your parents for years and observed the way they boast about you, I can assure you they are very proud of you just as you are. No matter what accolades your mother may have given you that day, though, ultimately you are the only one who can validate you. You have to be able to accept that imperfections are a part of life and that they are not a reason for personal attack but rather a reality for us all."

Like many women, Rebecca had found a scapegoat in her mother and tried to blame her for a perceived personal attack. Mothers are instructors who have a need to correct, discipline, and guide. Most have no desire to unleash a load of guilt on the children they have birthed. However, someone with a mental tie based on the desire for perfection can easily see such suggestions as criticism. This exchange between Rebecca and her mother was the catalyst for an outburst that produced the activation energy she needed to see that changing her mind-set was necessary for her to be free to enjoy life.

Who is your scapegoat when you feel personally attacked? Is it your husband, your children, your boss? Or once you really think about it, do the judgments start long before they make the first comment? Let's say you cook your son's favorite spaghetti meal. You serve it up and he says, "This tastes different, Mom." If your first response is anger, chances are you had a preconceived mind-set of what he would say. Your expectations were not met, and you responded as if you were wounded—with anger.

As you can see, self-judgment can work both ways, with either a prideful root or a self-defeatist root. A perfectionist mind-set says you are not allowed to have an off day, so if someone confronts you then that person is the one with the problem. The flip side of this scenario would be if you happened to be out of the garlic you normally put in the spaghetti and were hoping no one would notice, or at least have the decency not to say anything! Yes, some days the spaghetti will be magnificent. But when it's not, just shrug it off, forgive yourself, and forgive the innocent who voiced a rebuke.

Transition—*Stretched to the Max but Rebounding with Grace*

What do you perceive as your biggest flaw? What is it about you that you wish you could change? If it's a habit like smoking that can endanger your health and the health of those around you, you have a valid reason to work toward changing it. But if it's the way you look or the way you laugh or some other unique quality about yourself, it does not have to continue being a source of discontentment. Instead of launching another personal attack condemning yourself for all of your flaws and imperfections, use that energy to step through the door of grace.

The transition state in the mental tie of perfectionism is like a teeter-totter, with the things you do well on one side and your perceived failures on the other side. Our emotions sit at the center point, waiting to see which side the balance will favor. On the good days when we feel we meet most of our expectations, we are elated; on the bad days when we do not accomplish our goals, we are dissatisfied. Grace is the equalizing force that keeps the scales in balance. It has the ability to cover not only those things we excel at but also those things we struggle with.

If you cannot bake a cake that will win awards, obtain the grace to make cupcakes instead. If you do not have a designer's eye for decoration, obtain the grace to accept the advice of a professional. If you do not have time to do the dishes before you go to bed, obtain the grace to forgive yourself. No matter what the perceived flaw, grace has the potential to shade in the missing parts to display an acceptable end result.

Perfection is not the goal for our lives. Balance, peace, joy, happiness, and love are the goals we should be seeking. These qualities are the by-products of a life released from the mental bondage of self-criticism. You can live with contentment while being perfectly imperfect.

4

I Am Perfectly Imperfect

Perfection is like an imaginary box setting boundaries within our lives. Like all boxes, the four supporting sides dictate its capacity. The four elements that limit perfection are our past experience, our present knowledge, our future expectations, and our perceptions about God. Our idea of perfection is limited by our past experience of how others finished a task. It is restricted by our present knowledge of how to accomplish the task. It is bound by the future expectation of how we would like to finish the task. Lastly, our knowledge of who God is limits our interpretation of perfection. For example, if I asked you to define your perfect job you may think of someone who is currently working in that field. Your expectations would be limited by your present knowledge of how that person functions within that position. When you dictate how to complete a task based on your past, present, and future expectations, you limit God's ability to show you what he is able to do in your life.

The definition of perfection is to finish without a flaw. Perfection implies there is a right way and a wrong way to complete each goal; there is one route to excellence; there are no allowances for interpretation, no creative freedoms, no liberties to take, and no opportunities for growth. Perfection closes the door on the boundless possibilities given to you in the Word of God.

Breaking out of this mental box depends on an understanding of Psalm 119:96, which tells us that "Even perfection has its limits, but your commands have no limit." This verse discusses two key points. The first part implies that nothing and no one on earth is perfect. Only God is perfect. The second part of the verse implies that only the truths of the Bible have no limit. Scripture alone has the ability to produce a perfect effect within our lives and hearts. It does not matter how much you practice, how hard you strive, how much you spend in the pursuit of perfection—it will always remain a distant moving target, an unobtainable goal. Perfection within our lives can only be extracted from the truth of God's Word. Time spent meditating on principles that edify and equip produces growth within your spirit that allows new vision, new dreams, and new concepts. It gives you the ability to break free from the confines of perfectionism and move into the open space of excellence.

The Pursuit of Excellence

Instead of pursuing an elusive level of perfection, we would save ourselves a lot of disappointment and discouragement if we pursued excellence. Excellence goes beyond boundaries and limits. It is a concept that is open for exploration. It allows for individualized levels of excelling and calls us to go beyond our past experiences into uncharted territory. It surpasses prior expectations. Excellence is not confined to certain areas of life. It encompasses your career, your relationships, your personal health, and every choice you must make. You must establish an attitude of excellence to help foster your day-to-day decisions. Small tweaks in our performance culminate in excellence. It is easier for me to grab fast food on the way home for my children, but with twenty minutes of preparation and a decent Crock-Pot, I can pursue excellence by providing a meal with a higher nutritional content. Daily I can choose to complete various projects halfheartedly, or I can give them my undivided attention for a period of time and achieve a better outcome. Excellence requires allocating your resources to those areas of your life where you have the potential to exceed your prior accomplishments.

In the pursuit of excellence, it's important that you refrain from a sense of competition and reject the desire to revert back to a state of unhealthy comparisons. Otherwise, instead of excelling and trying to do your personal best, it becomes easier to just do better than someone else. Everyone has a different potential in which to excel. What may be easy for one person may be very difficult for someone else. For example, if you have a talent for art and base your level of excellence on my attempt at a masterpiece, you will definitely not live up to your full potential.

Ecclesiastes 9:10 encourages us to do whatever work we have before us with all of our strength. Excellence requires an effort on your part, but the rewards are many. It improves your self-esteem, builds your self-confidence, ushers in positive feedback from others, and leads to success. Excellence is an inward competition with yourself. There are no losers, only winners, since you are the only participant involved. It requires a desire to be better tomorrow as you apply what you have learned today. Excellence is matching your experience with your potential. With each new level of success you become more in tune with your personal capabilities. You can assess your strengths and weaknesses to help foster an even greater advancement of your personal best as God works within these areas.

The Power of Weakness

There is power in your weakness. Everyone has areas of weakness, but most of us try to cover them up. Unfortunately, when you spend a lifetime trying to hide your shortcomings from acquaintances, family, and friends, it becomes just as easy to try to hide them from God. God alone has the ability to unleash power through your weaknesses; when they become a source of insecurity and shame, you limit that power.

Knowing your weaknesses is the first step to releasing this power within your life. Identify those areas that require more of your time and reserves. Identify those things that cause you to become easily irritated. What activities make you want to run and hide? What phobias hinder you? Do you have a fear of speaking to crowds? Do you have a tendency to procrastinate? Does the word *patience* make you cringe? Are you easily angered? Have you had problems getting motivated?

Once you identify those areas of weakness within your life, you allow God the opening through which he can begin to infuse the power of his Word. You cannot change what you will not confront. You must address weaknesses, but they need not become a source of self-condemnation. They are areas of limitation that are awaiting a divine release. God is willing and able to breathe strength into the weak areas of your life. The power within your weaknesses has an unlimited potential as your weaknesses become God's personal projects. He assumes all rights to them and will use them for his glory. When you see your weaknesses growing in strength and power, you become fully aware of God's energy alive and flowing through those areas. Weaknesses are a wonderful asset. From glory to glory, watch as God uses your weaknesses to reveal his power.

Progress Now, Perfection Later

Can you imagine what life would be like if perfection was actually an attainable goal? What would you do after you were perfect? Where would you go after you reached the pinnacle? The only place to go would be down. Imperfection is actually for your benefit. Your imperfections make it possible for you to continue to move from glory to glory. You cannot move upward if you are already at the top. Do not allow yourself to see your weaknesses and imperfections as something to feel ashamed of. They are actually for a purpose and are universal to us all. We may not all have the same weaknesses, but we all have weaknesses, and that's how God planned it.

God does not expect you to be perfect. From the moment you were born into a world of crime, hate, selfishness, and injustice, the likelihood of your reaching perfection dropped to zero percent. Perfection is not the goal on earth; it is God's goal for your heavenly future. Your life is a progressive journey. There will be times of success and times of failure. There will be times of faith and times of doubt. There will be moments of joy and moments of fear. You cannot maneuver this obstacle course we call life and expect to finish the race perfectly. The goal is not to finish perfectly, but rather to learn and grow along the journey. The goal is progress in your areas of weakness so that each day you begin to look more like the person God sees when he looks at you.

Expulsion—*Dynamic Interference Required*

Insecurities have a way of laying deep roots in our souls. These roots spread in our spirits and tighten around our emotions. Fear accompanies them and can cause lagging productivity as it immobilizes further progress. The opposite of insecurity is security. The definition of security is being free from harm. It is a stable condition where there is freedom from the fear of uncertainty.

The Word of God is our security. It provides the freedom to rise above limitations to new points of excelling. It defeats fear as faith and hope arise to conquer the past and to stake claim on a better present and future. Allow these Scriptures to reveal to you who is truly perfect and how he is able to work within your imperfections.

- God alone is perfect.

He is the Rock, His work is perfect; For all His ways are justice, A God of truth and without injustice; Righteous and upright is He.

Deuteronomy 32:4 NKJV

- God's will for my life is perfect.

God's way is perfect. All the LORD's promises prove true. He is a shield for all who look to him for protection.

2 Samuel 22:31

- God does not expect me to be perfect.

All of us have sinned and fallen short of God's glory. But God treats us much better than we deserve, and because of Christ Jesus, he freely accepts us and sets us free from our sins.

Romans 3:23–24

- God cares enough to find me in my place of insecurity.

I will search for my lost ones who strayed away, and I will bring them safely home again. I will bandage the injured and strengthen the weak.

Ezekiel 34:16

- God wants to speak to me through his Word.

So then faith comes by hearing, and hearing by the word of God.

Romans 10:17 NKJV

- God's promises are my security.

God cannot tell lies! And so his promises and vows are two things that can never be changed. We have run to God for safety. Now his promises should greatly encourage us to take hold of the hope that is right in front of us.

Hebrews 6:18 CEV

- God understands my weaknesses.

Jesus understands every weakness of ours, because he was tempted in every way that we are. But he did not sin!

Hebrews 4:15 CEV

- God has made provisions to cover each weakness.

In certain ways we are weak, but the Spirit is here to help us. For example, when we don't know what to pray for, the Spirit prays for us in ways that cannot be put into words.

Romans 8:26 CEV

- God works through my weaknesses to reveal his power.

"My grace is all you need. My power works best in weakness." So now I am glad to boast about my weaknesses, so that the power of Christ can work through me.

2 Corinthians 12:9

- I can overcome my weaknesses with God's power.

I can do all things through Christ who strengthens me.

Philippians 4:13 NKJV

- Excellence is how I give thanks to God.

And whatever you do or say, do it as a representative of the Lord Jesus, giving thanks through him to God the Father.

Colossians 3:17

- Excellence is not an excuse for self-neglect.

It is useless to get up early and stay up late in order to earn a living. God takes care of his own, even while they sleep.

Psalm 127:2 CEV

- God is the source of my strengths.

God is my strength and power, and He makes my way perfect.

2 Samuel 22:33 NKJV

- Trusting in God will increase my strength.

He gives power to the weak and strength to the powerless. Even youths will become weak and tired, and young men will fall in exhaustion. But those who trust in the LORD will find

new strength. They will soar high on wings like eagles. They
will run and not grow weary. They will walk and not faint. .

Isaiah 40:29–31

• God is perfecting me for his future glory.

The LORD will perfect that which concerns me; Your mercy,
O LORD, endures forever; Do not forsake the works of Your
hands.

Psalm 138:8 NKJV

Detachment—*Cut the Ties (Snip, Snip)*

I have not yet reached my goal, and I am not perfect. But
Christ has taken hold of me. So I keep on running and strug-
gling to take hold of the prize. My friends, I don't feel that I
have already arrived. But I forget what is behind, and I struggle
for what is ahead. I run toward the goal, so that I can win
the prize of being called to heaven. This is the prize that God
offers because of what Christ Jesus has done. All of us who
are mature should think in this same way. And if any of you
think differently, God will make it clear to you. But we must
keep going in the direction that we are now headed.

Philippians 3:12–16 CEV

I would have to agree with Paul; I am not perfect. I do not
work out at the gym daily. My kids are well acquainted with
every cartoon that has graced a time slot on the Disney Chan-
nel. Sometimes we omit study time to play video games as
a family. I indulge in chocolate way more than I should. I've
been known to make a meal out of just one of the six food
groups. I find myself chatting on Facebook when I should
be doing more productive things like the mounting stack
of laundry. I have the patience of a three-year-old . . . well,

maybe a six-year-old. I am not a picture of perfection. But Jesus has so changed my life, my mind, and my desires that I keep trying each day to do better than I did the day before.

I have not arrived at where I would like to see myself spiritually, physically, or emotionally; but like you, I intend to continue working toward my goals. I am putting away past fatal mind-sets, past insecurities, and past failures, and I am reaching toward what God has ahead for me. Jesus has paved the way for me to have "a rich and satisfying life" (John 10:10). God is making his plan for my life clear to me each day. I am allowing his Word to dynamically intervene in my circumstances. My only goal now is to progress toward excellence in all I do and trust that he will complete my perfection in heaven.

LIE #2

Envy

5

I Would Be Happy Too If I Had Her Life

The laptop let out an annoyingly loud beep as the stilettos crashed into the keyboard. Gina couldn't care less that her miniskirt was up to her hips as her legs rested on the desk. Everyone else had headed home hours ago. Her office was littered with piles of discarded proposals on every workable surface area. She leaned back into the cushioned seat of her office chair and closed her eyes. She could feel the mounting tension and weight of the day as she breathed out a heavy sigh.

How was she going to meet this deadline? There was no way humanly possible to complete the task she had at hand, no way to make this work without asking for an extension. *Failure* was the word that came to mind when she envisioned asking Mr. Davidson for additional time to work with the marketing department. How was she ever going to convince him that she was worthy of becoming an executive director if she couldn't deliver on such an important project? She knew that she had to have something concrete to show him by their weekly meeting tomorrow.

The following day's schedule was filled to capacity, but Gina had to find a way to fit in an emergency meeting with her team. Dissecting every hour down to the minute resulted in a small thirty-minute block of time that would have to suffice. A few clicks later and the email was off, notifying everyone of the impromptu meeting. There was no way she was going to get passed by on this upcoming promotion. If she had to give her entire team a kick in the behind to get them motivated, then so be it.

Moving from her reclining position, Gina headed down the corridor toward the elevator to go home. The elevator light was stationary at the twelfth floor for an extended period of time. She noted the irony of it as she felt like the elevator of her career and life was stuck too.

⚬✕⚬

Gina had never been particularly good at networking, nor was she especially gifted at climbing the corporate ladder. But one thing she had in abundance was motivation. Growing up in less-than-stellar conditions had given her an appreciation for the process of success. She was not afraid of hard work. If she needed to work extra hours to get the job done, she was prepared to sacrifice whatever she had to in order to grab the bigger prize ahead. Gina knew someone was going to move to the executive suite, and she was determined this was going to be her year.

Her corporate climb had not been a sprint to the finish, but rather a slow and steady progression upward. From junior associate to associate to senior associate to managing director, Gina pulled herself one rung at a time toward her goal. With each step up she put in even more hours after work and spent even more time away from the people she loved. As if something internal was pulling her toward a determined end, Gina could not rest until she was an executive director. Each inch closer to her goal sparked a flame that burned in her mental vision and left a smoky haze over everything that had transpired before it.

"Please tell me someone has something better than this," Gina pleaded as she glanced at the faces of her team around the conference table.

Never in her time at the firm had she felt so unprepared for a meeting with her superior. Not one of the ideas on the table was good enough for her to present to Mr. Davidson. It was unavoidable. She would have to ask for an extension.

Through the window of the adjacent conference room, Gina spotted Jill Anderson's signature stance as she leaned over a colleague to review a proposal. Jill was ten years Gina's junior and had already accomplished Gina's goals. Jill seemed to skip up the corporate ladder. Everything about Jill infuriated Gina—her voice, her laugh, the clothes she wore, and most of all, that insidious smile she always seemed to have on her face.

It must be easy to smile all day when your life is a dessert tray filled with delicacies, Gina mused.

"How's the project going, Gina?" questioned Mr. Davidson as she slid into the chair across from his desk.

"Slowly," confessed Gina. "We're going to need additional time to complete the marketing proposal. I am so disappointed that we weren't able to meet the deadline."

"No big deal. Jill just asked for an extension also. Apparently her division is having a creative slump as well this month. I just gave them an additional month and will grant the same to your team. By the way, great job on the Morrison account. Your name came up numerous times last week at the executive committee meeting." Mr. Davidson smiled as he escorted her to the door.

The smile Gina flashed him as she walked out the door merely veiled her mental calculations, for she was computing the overtime needed to complete this project early. As elated as she was to hear that her name had come up during the discussion for the promotion, compliments only made her work harder. She knew that if she could beat Jill at meeting the deadline, she would be a shoe-in for that executive position. She could envision herself moving into the vacant executive corner suite.

No time to celebrate now, she thought. *I've got work to do.*

Lie #2: I Would Be Happy Too If I Had Her Life

"The grass is always greener on the other side of the fence" is the old adage that best depicts this lie. Looking at life through a single focus can make someone else's life seem appealing. It's when you zoom in for the close-up that you really get a chance to see what's at the core of a matter. Every life has its peaks and valleys.

On my drive to work I pass some amazingly lush hills. These beautiful landscapes appear immaculately manicured with soft, fluffy acres of grass. I often imagine taking off my shoes to wiggle my toes in this picturesque flowing river of green. One morning while looking for a quiet place to reflect, I decided to venture into one of these grassy oases. But when I pulled up to the spot, I could not believe my eyes. There was beautiful green grass, but weeds and numerous bare patches were mixed with it. Distance has the deceptive ability to make things appear much better than they actually are.

Similarly, most of us do not display the negative or difficult aspects of our lives for all to see. We often only show a single image that we desire to portray. For example, if you are considered a smart student, you may be quick to show off your As but less likely to discuss that you stayed up all night studying to earn them. If you are known for making beautifully creative cakes, you will be elated to bring your creation to the women's brunch but reluctant to tell them that the first two soufflés fell in the center. If you are the Sunday school teacher, you are more than willing to pray for a member whose husband was found cheating but you would never ask for prayer for your husband's pornography addiction.

When you peer at others' lives through the small window they allow you, it is easy to become envious over the blessings you see. It may even seem like God is playing favorites, pouring blessings and favor on their lives beyond what you feel they deserve. It may seem that they came by the successes in their lives so easily, while you have to work harder to get to the same point. Why is their grass so green and yours always looks so unkempt? Could it be that your vantage point has distorted your vision?

All grass has weeds; you just have to get close enough to see them. So rather than focus on someone else's lawn, you must take care to focus on the grass on your side of the fence. What do you have inside of you that you have not cultivated with life-giving nutrients? What growth in your life are you stunting by trampling it underfoot? Is it possible that the landscape of your life would look a lot better if you spent more time nurturing and fertilizing your bare spots back to health?

Illumination—*Peek Inside Yourself*

Personal advancement and achievement are admirable and necessary for fulfillment. Whether your career takes you into the boardroom or into the laundry room is irrelevant; the only important aspect of your career and life is that it brings you some level of personal satisfaction. If your satisfaction level is at an all-time low, it's time to get a closer look at what's bringing you down.

Do any of the following statements describe you?

- I measure myself based on others' expectations of me.
- I judge my self-worth based on the validation of others.
- I work harder than most to get ahead in my career.
- I choose my purchases based on how they will look to others rather than on my personal needs or desires.
- When I enter a room, I look at how others are dressed to see if I fit in.
- I compete with the person beside me at the gym to see who can exercise harder.
- When I have a performance review, I am very upset if I don't get the top ranking.
- If I accept my current level of success, I will not work as hard to advance myself.
- I get upset when I hear of someone else getting something I want.
- I feel guilty if I take time off from work.
- I feel life comes easy for others.
- The meal choices of my dining companions always seem to look tastier than mine.
- I often desire what I see that others have.
- I feel that other people enjoy their lives more than I do.
- I second-guess my choices because I fear I may be missing a better option.
- I measure my success by the success of others.

This mental tie revolves around fatalistic comparisons with others that leave you with a sense of loss. If you always feel as if you get the short end of the deal, eventually you become judgmental and bitter. Bitterness has the ability to seep deeply within your soul. Like yeast, it slowly expands its capacity to permeate numerous areas of your life. As bitterness works its way through the dense areas of your interpersonal relationships and career, it consumes your joy and peace and excretes the by products of fear and anger.

The longer this mental tie ferments within your life, the more its network continues to strengthen and bubble over into mundane areas. Suddenly you get upset not only over the raise your co-worker received but also over the fact that her lunch order came with more fries than yours. The only way to halt this progressive assault on your emotional peace is to cease feeding bitterness what it needs to survive.

Activation—*Change Is Hard Work and It May Involve Sweat*

Life should be a series of celebrations as you move from glory to glory. Stop at each point along your destined route to enjoy the blessings. Move from a place of always competing to a place of congratulating. Congratulating someone's accomplishments opens your heart and mind to be receptive to celebrate with that person without condemning yourself. Competing puts up a wall that will ultimately make one of you the winner and one the loser. And even if you win that particular battle, you lose mentally because it only serves to put more pressure on you to win next time. This mentality leads to a cycle of continuous striving without any outlet to express happiness, joy, and contentment.

The hardest part of personal growth is doing an inventory of your assets. It is easy to see the good in others but much more difficult to see similar attributes within yourself. Often your own uniqueness will make your contribution completely different from the person you admire, yet your input is still equally valuable and needed. The greatest loss to humanity comes when unique treasures try to dull their shine to fit in with the crowd rather than display their brilliance for all to behold.

Activate your desire to see your life in a new way. Look for your personal triumphs each day. Keep a journal of past victories as a reminder that the grass is pretty green on your side as well. Make a habit of identifying blessings the moment they enter your atmosphere. Someone pulling out of the best parking space at the mall the second you arrive equals a blessed you. A friend dropping by to take you out to lunch also equals a blessed you. If you look for blessings, you will often find that your day is sprinkled with them. Use these reminders as the water needed to refresh your parched mental ground. As you saturate that hard brittle ground of bitterness, it will begin to soften and break up, allowing new life to spring forth.

Transition—*Stretched to the Max but Rebounding with Grace*

Breaking this mental tie has the potential to change your entire personality. Bitter people are not fun to be around. Listening to someone's woe-is-me story can quickly turn a pleasant encounter into a depressed, awkward exchange. In contrast, people who are content to enjoy the journey to personal success and not just the destination are much more fun as life's traveling companions.

The transition state in breaking the mental tie of unhealthy comparisons requires self-acceptance. It requires accepting your life as an individualized itinerary booked specifically with you in mind by God himself. He controls your arrival and departure dates, but he leaves you the freedom to personalize your travel agenda based on your personal choices. Your days can be chock-full of envy, jealousy, bitterness, and depression. Or your days can be filled with peace, love, joy, happiness, and the blessings of God as you accept the itinerary by trusting him in faith.

Self-acceptance is the ability to appreciate, support, and validate who you are and where you are at any moment in time. This includes those areas that you would like to change. It gives you the latitude to be yourself rather than who others expect you to be. It acknowledges your self-worth and gives you the freedom to be open and vulnerable without judgment.

In the opening of this chapter, Gina's resume is a testimony of blessing after blessing. Her advancement within her company is to be commended. But why is it that she cannot seem to stop for even one moment to bask in the sunshine of a much-deserved compliment? In one word: motivation. For Gina the driving force behind her success has been the need to get to the next level. Her lack of self-acceptance has become her motivating factor.

The way Gina sees it, allowing herself to appreciate her current level of success would be the same as giving up her dream to become an executive director. She incorrectly believes that if she accepts where she is, she will not work as hard getting to her goals. So rather than enjoying the journey, she has become envious and jealous of her co-worker who has learned that she can remain motivated without self-condemnation.

For Gina, judging herself unfavorably has been the motivation for the success in her life. Feeling bad about her current position is her catalyst to work harder and longer. Although a feasible means to an end, it often backfires by breeding a lack of self-esteem. So while she may ultimately reach the intended level of success, she will have a difficult time learning how to stay motivated to maintain it. If you are only happy when you reach your end goals, what percentage of your life is actually spent living?

Take the time to enjoy the journey and not just the destination. Utilize your time traveling from where you are to where you want to be so that you become comfortable with your uniqueness. Learn to treasure each victory as an accomplishment within itself. Opportunities for unhealthy comparisons will arise, but a mentality of self-acceptance can overcome them. Your personal path to happiness and wholeness will have a heavenly fingerprint upon it specific to you. There is no need to put your life on hold until you meet a certain goal. Celebrate life daily. What accomplishment do you need to celebrate today?

6

I Am Too Unique for Comparisons

As I am writing this chapter, snow is falling outside my window. Its accumulation paints the surrounding landscape a beautiful white portrait. I am amazed at the different sizes of the snowflakes—from tiny, powdery fine ones to some the size of my morning bran flakes. Each flake gracefully takes a specific path on its descent to earth. Some will end up on tree limbs, others will get rolled into snowballs and snowmen, and still others will sit undisturbed upon rooftops awaiting the appearance of the sun. Each flake is unique in appearance, destination, and purpose. Each is handcrafted by God.

You are just as unique as one of these divine creations. The hand of God crafted your complexion, height, eye color, hair color, and bone structure. Beyond the outward appearance, God has inwardly crafted you to be unique. He has directed circumstances and events to help lead you into the specific destination he desires. He has a specific purpose in mind for your life and a plan to help you fulfill your destiny. Like the cascade of snowflakes outside, our lives can take us to places we may not have chosen for ourselves. I can imagine a tiny snowflake high up on a power line complaining, "I would rather be on the ground enjoying the snowball fight below." Or another snowflake reluctantly getting shoveled into a pile and complaining, "Put me up on the roof so I can be left alone!"

As comical as this seems, can you imagine the chaos that would ensue? Thankfully, snowflakes do not compare themselves to other snowflakes, nor do they try to look identical to those around them. They drift along on the wind currents and fulfill their potential in whatever place they land. They rest in the Creator's plan, content as his unique creations to follow his will that works all things for good. As human beings created in God's image, we can be certain we are of far greater worth than snowflakes. We would be wise to follow their example, however, by being secure in who we are as individuals and confident in the Creator's perfect will for our lives.

Television, magazines, and even the Bible can be sources for women to find someone to envy. Proverb 14:30 states, "A peaceful heart leads to a healthy body; jealousy is like cancer in the bones." Recent studies show that there is a "paradox of declining female happiness." In a 2009 *American Economic Journal* article titled "The Paradox of Declining Female Happiness," economists Betsey Stevenson and Justin Wolfers show that although women today have more opportunities in their careers, their overall happiness is much less than women enjoyed thirty years ago. The study suggests that women's newfound freedom has led to dwindling joy. This lack of joy, in my opinion, is not an issue of freedom but of the mental tie associated with unhealthy comparisons. If I am always striving to be like the woman in the office beside me, it will cause unnecessary stress in my life. Over time this competitive nature will spread like a cancer into other areas of your life, including your happiness. Learning how to appreciate your uniqueness is vital to a life of freedom and contentment.

Defining Moments

If I were to ask you to write a paragraph to define who you are, what would you say? Would you start with a list of your accomplishments? Would your paragraph focus on your career, your family, your appearance, or your personality? Upon which aspects of your life do you place the most value for defining who you are? What events in your life do you allow to define you?

How you define yourself determines what areas of your life you allow others to access. If you define yourself as a homemaker, you may find it very easy to discuss topics related to the home but shy away from sharing the song you wrote last night during your time of prayer. Similarly, if you have a reputation for being a poised businesswoman, it could be very difficult to share your needs during times you require help. Life has many defining moments that leave an imprint on how we view ourselves. When your view of yourself becomes narrow, it decreases your ability to accept the unique attributes that you have to offer.

When you attempt to define yourself, you separate your life into finite areas: you become either the businesswoman or the homemaker, shy or outgoing, beautiful or average, poised or emotional. Once you internalize these classifications about yourself, eventually you will begin to portray this identity to others. Over time it is easy to become locked into an identity that is too small for what God wants to do in your life. You are too diverse to allow yourself to become boxed into categories. What lies behind the categorical doors you've closed in the past? Isn't it time to become acquainted with *you* again?

The Voices in the Crowd

It's easier for others to pin you in a specific category than to spend the time needed to learn more about you. In the course of a day I interact with over fifty different people. I don't have the time or the resources to personally know each person I come into contact with, so it's convenient to group people. When I have a question about computers, I have specific people I turn to for help. When I need prayer, I wouldn't think of calling the atheists I know but rather the group of ladies with whom I can be vulnerable. It is natural to want to catalog and simplify life as much as possible, but you must take the time to learn who you are and what you want out of life. External voices may plant the seed, but ultimately you get the final vote. Avoid accepting others' categorizations as fact. Do not be content to remain within the categories in which life has tried to box you.

The voices in the crowd may tell you that it's impossible to find work in today's economy, but your internal voice may be telling you it's time for a change. Your friends may be telling you to stay in your place when your heart is telling you to pursue your love of music. Fear may be telling you to stop dreaming. Grief may be telling you to turn back now before you lose something else. Anxiety may be keeping you up at night as it recites a negative report. Shame may be convincing you that you do not deserve more out of life. What voices are controlling your decisions? What voices have you allowed to dictate your next steps? Many voices in the crowd can confuse the voice of truth that God wants you to hear.

71

Complex by Design

Have you ever wondered why there are so many elements to the Proverbs 31 woman? This model woman has more titles and activities than many of us would ever care to have. I've always wondered why God put this picture of "superwomanhood" into the Bible. It has always struck me as an impossible expectation to try to live up to. I have since come to realize that I am not supposed to try to *be* her; rather, this picture of complexity is God's way of showing me that I do not have to be limited to a trade, a position, a relationship, or anything else. I am free to explore my repertoire of internal gifting without restraints. I am complex by design.

You are a complex individual knitted together piece by piece by a loving God. He created you with your own unique talents, likes, and desires. He knows you better than you know yourself. He sees you as he created you, not as you or others have defined you. You are an exclusive, one-of-a-kind treasure that has yet to be fully explored. You are too unique to compare to any other. How can you compare the incomparable? No one has your distinct personal characteristics. No one has your exact personality. No one has your precise set of experiences. You are an authentic heavenly masterpiece worthy of inspiring thanks to God. "Thank you for making me so wonderfully complex! Your workmanship is marvelous—how well I know it" (Ps. 139:14).

Hidden Talents

What talents have you been hiding? Your talent will not look like anyone else's. If you are a singer, you will not sound exactly like anyone else. If you are a chef, your dishes will not taste exactly like another's. This is what makes talents

72

special—they are God-given endowments in your life. There are many great musicians; what makes them unique are the intrinsic variations in the quality of their voices. There are many great artists; what separates them is their level of originality.

Talent is an innate ability to excel at something. It's the things that come naturally to you. The strange thing about talent is that it must be revealed. Inside of you could reside the ability to play the piano like no one else, but if you never allow yourself the chance to explore your musical abilities, you may never know that this gift lies within you. You could have a knack for creative writing or for speaking encouragement into difficult situations. Your God-given gifts don't have to be musical or communicative either; they can include your propensity to charity work and acts of compassion. To find your hidden talents you must first determine what is blinding your ability to see them.

A haze of mental debris can bury your talents. When your mind becomes clouded by fear, indifference, shame, regret, and self-doubt, it becomes impossible to see clearly. Such feelings must be cleared out to allow your gifts to rise to the surface. A lifestyle of constant busyness can also obscure your gifts. Time can work for you or against you. If it seems as if you never have enough time to do new things, it is unlikely that you will discover hidden talents. Talents are like treasures hidden along the course of your life. If your course never takes you into new areas of experience, you will not have opportunities to discover those treasures.

Allow the voice of God to awaken the gifts within you. Scripture has the ability to speak into our lives. It is as effective today in its power to change lives as it was when it was written. Expect the removal of layers of debris as truth restores your spirit, mind, and soul. Allow new life to be breathed into your dead places that are in need of resurrection.

Expulsion—*Dynamic Interference Required*

Choose to listen to the voice of God through the truth of his Word. For every mental tie, the Scriptures have the power to heal the wounded areas of your life. Allow these words to penetrate deep into your soul's injuries. As they breathe life into places that have lain dormant, let your faith arise to embrace the truths you learn about yourself. There are hidden treasures within you that you have yet to uncover. The only way to retrieve them is to spend time exploring the deep and secret recesses of your soul. Spend some time in solitude as these words from God uncover buried potential. Your efforts may start as a small seed, but his words are the water it needs to grow into maturity. Your family, your friends, your loved ones, your community—and most importantly, *you*—will benefit when you discover who you are in God.

- There are treasures from God within me.

I will give you treasures hidden in dark and secret places. Then you will know that I, the LORD God of Israel, have called you by name.

Isaiah 45:3 CEV

- God wants to help me discover my gifts.

If you don't know what you're doing, pray to the Father. He loves to help. You'll get his help, and won't be condescended to when you ask for it.

James 1:5 Message

- The gifts and talents God has placed in my life cannot be taken from me, but they can be hidden from my view.

For God's gifts and His call are irrevocable. [He never with-draws them when once they are given, and He does not change His mind about those to whom He gives His grace or to whom He sends His call.]

Romans 11:29 AMP

- Gifts are to use, not store.

Having gifts (faculties, talents, qualities) that differ according to the grace given us, let us use them.

Romans 12:6 AMP

- I have at least one special gift from God I can use to help others.

Each of you has been blessed with one of God's many won-derful gifts to be used in the service of others. So use your gift well.

1 Peter 4:10 CEV

- My unique gifting reveals God's power working in my life.

However, we possess this precious treasure [the divine Light of the Gospel] in [frail, human] vessels of earth, that the grandeur and exceeding greatness of the power may be shown to be from God and not from ourselves.

2 Corinthians 4:7 AMP

- The gifts God has deposited within me have value.

What you receive from me is more valuable than even the finest gold or the purest silver.

Proverbs 8:19 CEV

- It is never too late to start anew.

For we are God's masterpiece. He has created us anew in Christ Jesus, so we can do the good things he planned for us long ago.

Ephesians 2:10

- God has a good future planned for me.

"For I know the plans I have for you," says the LORD. "They are plans for good and not for disaster, to give you a future and a hope."

Jeremiah 29:11

- I am precious to God, and he wants me to be happy.

You are precious to me, and so I will rebuild your nation. Once again you will dance for joy and play your tambourines.

Jeremiah 31:4 CEV

- God wants me to succeed.

And I am certain that God, who began the good work within you, will continue his work until it is finally finished on the day when Christ Jesus returns.

Philippians 1:6

- Surrounding my life with God's Word leads to success.

Study this Book of Instruction continually. Meditate on it day and night so you will be sure to obey everything written in it. Only then will you prosper and succeed in all you do.

Joshua 1:8

Detachment—*Cut the Ties (Snip, Snip)*

It would be great if I could prescribe someone a single dose of blood pressure medication and cure her hypertension. But one pill only has the potential to effect change on the day she takes it. If she omits a dose, the symptoms of elevated blood pressure will return. The only way someone can get off of the pill is to drastically change her body's chemistry, either though sustained weight loss or regular exercise.

Similarly the Scriptures above can begin to effect change the very first day you meditate on them, but for lasting change you must internalize them until they actually change you inwardly. They have the ability to drastically change the chemistry of your soul through sustained time with God and by exercising your trust in him.

Coming to terms with your own uniqueness means devoting time to becoming familiar with the gifts God has entrusted to you. It means a willingness on your part to break free from categories others have placed you in and from restrictions you have placed upon yourself. There are talents, gifts, and potential on the inside of you that you have yet to discover. You can reflect God's glory from the place he has allowed you to occupy. There is no need to compare your problems, your circumstances, your finances, or any other aspect of your life to another. You are too unique for comparisons. There is not one other person in the world like you, and that's exactly how God wants it.

LIE #3

Image

7

If I Do This, I Can Look Like That

As if the burning drops of sweat stinging her eyes were not enough, the rumbling in her stomach caused Natalie to stir from her mental vacation. The rhythmical hum of the treadmill was usually a calming sound to her; today though, it was more of a taunting nuisance. With a quick flick of her wristband, she averted the watery fountain attempting to overcome her vision just in time to see the 5:30 Zumba class leaving the gym. One by one they departed in trendy dancewear with their makeup intact and hair neatly pulled back. Each woman looked as if she had just stepped out of the pages of *Fitness* magazine. Natalie's reddish brown hair was piled high on her head in a messy bun, and the barrage of sweat pouring from her body had erased all traces of her foundation. Her efforts had soaked her pink "Search for a Cure" breast cancer awareness shirt. The machine's preprogrammed circuit began its incline, causing Natalie to push herself even more to keep up the pace. The heart rate monitor's flashing red numbers warned of an approaching peak heart rate. Panting for breath, Natalie's mind drifted back to one number: *eighteen*.

Two miles into her four-mile jog, Natalie pulled the emergency stop cord and bolted out of the crowded gym. She rushed past the group of gym divas lingering outside the classroom, almost knocking over one size 4 prima donna. Tears mixed with sweat as she quickly bounded up the stairs toward the women's locker room. She closed herself into the waiting embrace of the 110-degree steam room. The warmth released the tension in her mind as well as in her sore, achy muscles. Sitting there in her humidity-filled haven, she began to think back over the events of that day.

⟨⊙⟩⟨⊙⟩

"Sizes 12 and 18 are the only ones we have in those jeans, Ma'am," the sales associate informed Natalie as she handed her a size 18.

"I asked for a 14 or a 16," retorted Natalie.

"This brand tends to run small and I'm pretty good with guessing sizes," the associate said with a smile.

Natalie hesitated to try on the jeans. She had been dieting for the past three months, and the resulting twelve-pound loss was a disappointment for her. Despite her better judgment, she decided to treat herself to a new outfit in the hope it would motivate her to continue her weight loss efforts. She had always worn plus size clothes and was excited about shopping in the misses section for the first time in years. Her goal was to get down to a size 10. Natalie was well aware that she had not reached her destination, but she was confident that she could snugly fit into a size 14 or 16. She pulled on the size 18 to show herself how far she'd come, only to find out they fit perfectly. *Perfectly*!

Three months of depriving herself of her favorite Starbucks latte. Three months of sacrificing time with her family and friends to torture herself with hour-long sessions at the gym. Three months of calorie counting, bench pressing, stair stepping, and binge conquering had only resulted in a loss of one pound per week, dropping her down from 200 to 188 pounds. Twelve measly pounds for all that work! "It's not worth it," she concluded as she hung the repulsive size 18 jeans back on the hanger and left the store.

There was no doubt where she was headed. "One grande white chocolate mocha, please, with extra whipped cream," Natalie said to the barista at the coffee shop. The warmth from the drink caused a warming in her spirit, as if she had been reunited with a dear old friend.

Sitting there in the steam room, Natalie wondered why she had even come to the gym today. Was it guilt over her lapse? A punishment to work off her calorie-dense frothy beverage? Desperation to fit into those size ten jeans by her birthday? Whatever the reason, she was definitely regretting her decision.

"I hate this!" she yelled into the foggy abyss of steam, oblivious to the fact that she was not alone.

"I've never been a fan of the steam room either, but I hear it's great for your skin," a voice behind Natalie said, startling her.

"Oh! I didn't see you!" Natalie apologized. "I was actually referring to dieting, not the steam room."

The stream of steam was slowly clearing between cycles, allowing Natalie to get her first glimpse of her mystery companion. Leaning back against the walls of the steam room was a woman she had seen in the gym on many occasions. She had never spoken to the woman, but they always smiled at each other when they passed in the halls or out in the parking lot.

The two sat in silence for the remainder of their time to-gether. The stranger was the first to leave. Natalie waited a few minutes, then also left her mental incubation chamber. She loved how the stifling heat always made her feel much lighter, as if purging the toxins from her body also cleared the mental debris in her spirit.

"I think you're doing a pretty good job at dieting if you ask me," the stranger interjected.

Natalie caught a glimpse of the woman untangling her freshly washed hair in front of the mirror beside the showers. Unsure of how she would have any knowledge of her dieting failures or successes, Natalie was happy to hear something positive from anyone, even a complete stranger.

"Thanks, but I really stink at it. I haven't lost very much and I've been at it for a while."

"I've seen you working really hard during your workouts, and I know you've lost some weight since you joined the gym. I would guess you've lost a dress size or so, about ten or fifteen pounds."

"Twelve, to be exact, but what's twelve pounds when you have fifty to go?" mused Natalie.

"Twelve less you have to deal with!" exclaimed the stranger. "I work with a lot of women who are trying to lose weight, so if you feel you need some support or assistance, give me a call. I'm Saundra by the way." The woman smiled as she handed Natalie her business card and gathered her belong-ings to leave.

Natalie looked at the business card for a brief moment before throwing it into her gym bag as she headed for the shower stall. *I bet I could get down to a size 10 by summer if I had some diet pills,* she thought. She planned on making an appointment as soon as possible.

Lie #3: If I Do This, I Can Look Like That

> Each individual woman's body demands to be accepted on
> its own terms.
>
> Gloria Steinem

As a physician, I would love to see every woman within ten
pounds of her ideal weight. The problem with such a statement is that it requires a concrete definition of ideal body
weight. For some women it's the weight they were prior to
childbirth, for others it may be the weight at which they had
the fewest medical ailments, and for still others it may be the
weight at which they perceived they were the most attractive.
Whatever the motivating factor, the reality is that women
have become weight and dieting obsessed to the point where
it has become counterproductive.

Many women have entered my office looking for the latest medical advances on dieting and exercise. Armed with
testimonials about how one friend lost a hundred pounds on
diet XYZ and another shed her baby weight with the latest
miracle diet pill, each woman expects to be the next diet success story. Most are eager to reach their goals by any means
necessary, regardless of the effects on their health or sanity.

So every January 1 an unusually large number of female
patients present for a prescription appetite suppressant and
counseling on weight loss. At their follow-up weigh-in visit,
most have lost weight. However, as time passes, so does the
initial enthusiasm, and those inspirational pictures taped
to the refrigerator begin to seem like an unobtainable goal.

Many women subscribe to health-related magazines and
websites, receiving daily or monthly reminders to cut carbs
and increase activity. Pictures of thin, toned bodies lace each
reminder. Subconsciously we admire and covet these beautifully maintained bodies, causing us to do a mental inventory

83

of what we dislike about our own bodies: thighs too jiggly, hips too wide, tummy too soft, breasts too saggy, arms too floppy. Eventually you get so fed up with criticizing yourself that you finally make the decision to go on a diet. But rather than dieting for the sake of improved health, most of the ladies gracing the examination tables in my office want to lose weight for superficial reasons. Superficial reasons often end up with superficial results and an unhappy customer.

Once the person has made the decision to undergo a weight loss effort, she decides which diet program to follow and what exercises to incorporate. The latest trendy diet with the biggest promise as featured in the media is often the winner: lose thirty pounds in six weeks, have flatter abs in one month, drop a dress size in thirty days. I've found that the larger the media hype about a particular diet, the less likely its long-term success. Whether it's low carbs, no carbs, high protein, low fat, or some combination thereof, the fact remains that the results will not be the same for everyone.

Beware of any exercise or diet program that claims specific things, such as a specific amount of weight or a specific change guaranteed by following the program. It is a mental trap set to further your codependence with the billion-dollar weight loss industry. This mental tie works by setting a goal that you have no control over, but it gives you the illusion that if you follow Plan ABC you can meet the goal. The reality is that you have absolutely no control over your body's metabolic cycles, calorie usage efficiency, or muscle integrity, all of which determine the final outcome of any dieting venture.

God alone has retained the rights to what your body is capable of achieving. You can manipulate whether your body is in fat-burning or fat-storing mode, but when is the last time you were able to direct your excess fat to your cleavage instead of to your bottom? Have you ever attempted to lose fat in a specific spot? I recall trying a diet once to flatten my stomach. I followed this plan to the letter, including eating the exact foods on the sample menu plans, only to end up a size smaller with the same tummy. I should have been excited over my weight loss, but I was too busy beating myself up over not succeeding in losing my belly fat. This caused me to retreat to my own pity party complete with cake and ice cream. Have you ever visited the land of diet failure? In most cases, you didn't fail the diet but rather it failed to deliver what it promised.

> I've been on a diet for two weeks and all I've lost is fourteen days.
>
> Totie Fields

Illumination—*Peek Inside Yourself*

Embracing a healthy lifestyle and model of eating is an excellent undertaking for anyone who wants good health. Exercise is an excellent stress reliever and confidence booster. But if your time spent at the gym becomes a time to compare your buns to the buns of the woman on the StairMaster, you may need to further investigate what's holding you back from reaching your health goals.

Do any of the following statements describe you?

- I cringe whenever I see a picture of myself because I'm unhappy with how I look.
- My anxieties about how I look interfere with my ability to socially interact with others.
- The thinner I am, the better I like myself.
- I get angry at myself when I gain weight because I feel that I should have better self-control over what I eat.

- When people tell me I look good, I don't believe them.
- My anxieties about how I look interfere with my ability to enjoy sex.
- I say negative things about my appearance and point out my flaws when I talk to others.
- When I interact with an attractive woman, I feel intimidated and inferior.
- Shopping for clothes makes me upset because I feel that nothing I try on looks good on me.

The above statements originate from a posture of insecurity, a lack of confidence in your ability to stand your ground in a crowd. I am always amazed at how even a small amount of weight loss can cause a woman who has been hiding herself in baggy sweaters to all of a sudden become self-assured enough to wear the brightest clothes, cut her hair, and make a move toward being center stage. It is as if the weight loss has liberated her to express her personality, individuality, and uniqueness. Was she any less unique or interesting with the extra twenty pounds? Of course not, but failure has a way of making you feel inferior, and for many of us dieting failure has become the norm. When you have gained and lost the same thirty pounds, you eventually start to think that you are the problem. That type of negative self-talk adds an emotional weight that is far more deadly than the physical pounds.

Activation—*Change Is Hard Work and It May Involve Sweat*

Dieting has its own unique triggers for activation. An event such as an upcoming class reunion or a wedding can trigger the desire to lose weight. It can also be triggered by an abnormal lab result showing high cholesterol or diabetes. Or it can be the result of a general dissatisfaction with the status quo. I have found that when it comes to the personal battle with weight, those who get to the point where they no longer obsess about the specifics but embrace the journey have the most success at being happy with their weight loss efforts.

Transition—*Stretched to the Max but Rebounding with Grace*

As a former diet connoisseur, I can honestly say I have tried almost every diet plan on the market at some point in time. I would love to say that it was for my personal medical research, but in reality it was to shrink my thighs enough to fit into a size 6. I have learned many lessons along my weight loss journey and in my work with women who strive to lose weight. There are five questions I ask each of us to ponder before embarking on yet another diet program:

1. Why do you want to lose weight?
2. What short-term goals do you have for your weight loss plan?
3. What long-term goals do you have for your weight loss plan?
4. How will you define your successful plan?
5. When will you terminate your plan?

These five questions set the foundation for breaking down the old dieting mentality and incorporating a renewed outlook on weight management.

Why Do You Want to Lose Weight?

There are no absolute right or wrong answers to this question, but some answers predestine themselves for future downfall. Wanting to lose weight for an event or to improve a blood test can be the motivation needed to help some move toward better health. The problem is, that motivation (or activation energy) is not a sustaining energy. It is a short-lived burst of energy to spark the initial reaction. The person must apply a sustaining force over time for lasting results. The sustaining force of regular exercise, nutritionally dense foods, water, and spiritual rejuvenation can make even the most ludicrous diet plan a success story. This question is not intended to belittle someone's reason for weight loss, but rather to focus on the motivation for beginning a program and then differentiate that from the factors necessary for sustaining permanent weight loss.

What Short-Term Goals Do You Have for Your Weight Loss Plan?

Often the answer I get to this question is a dress size or an exact number of pounds lost. If someone is a hundred pounds overweight, getting to an ideal dress size can seem to take an eternity. Weight loss calculators can now spit out an exact date you should get to your weight loss goals based on your diet specifics. Unfortunately, most of this technology does not take into account that the natural ebb and flow of weight loss includes plateaus as the body attempts to stabilize itself. This can lead to a feeling of hope deferred or even of failure if you are relying on such calculations for your short-term goal. If your goal is to lose two pounds a week and you don't lose any this week, you are more likely to quit your program because it is not working according to the parameters you have established. Since you have no control over the exact number of pounds you can lose in a week, that figure should be a by-product of your goal. A more acceptable short-term goal would be to get twenty minutes of aerobic activity three days a week. This is a goal you have more control over. You can walk in place in the den if it's raining, chase the kids around the yard on a nice day, or race walk around the mall as you window shop. Goals should be something you have some level of control over. If you have no control over the outcome, it is no longer a goal but a wish.

What Long-Term Goals Do You Have for Your Weight Loss Plan?

You should base the long-term goals for your weight loss plan on the permanent life changes you need to maintain a healthy weight. Long-term goals should be the sustaining factors in place to carry out your plan until its expected end of weight loss. Again, your long-term goal should not be a dress size. I have seen many women battle mental demons trying to get into a dress size that is smaller than God intended their bodies to be. If you can only eat one meal a day, must exercise for hours every day, and have to take daily laxatives to maintain your current weight, then it is not the weight you were meant to be.

Your body is a gift given for you to enjoy. Eating and physical activity are both part of the freedom you have to express and receive joy within your body. Anything that robs you of your ability to move freely within the body you've been given is a form of bondage. Emotional eating, sedentary lifestyle, and food addictions all constrict your spirits with physical and mental weight. Learning how to recognize emotional triggers to eating is an example of a successful long-term goal that releases you from the confines of past dieting failures.

How Will You Define Your Successful Plan?

Defining success is mandatory for those trying to obtain it. How will you know when you can celebrate if you don't have an endpoint? This is the stage where you can incorporate numbers carefully. I urge patients to avoid sizes and to focus on weight ranges. Rather than having an exact weight or number of pounds lost, I find that ranges allow for greater freedom for success. Giving yourself a ten-pound range above and below your ideal number opens the door of accomplishment much wider than just saying you will be successful if you lose thirty pounds. It's often said that those last ten are the hardest to lose, but who says you really need to lose them? If you feel strong, vibrant, healthy, and happy, leave those last ten pounds alone and go celebrate your success!

When Will You Terminate Your Plan?

Yes, this is a trick question. For those who say they plan on terminating their plan once they reach X number of pounds lost, I quickly suggest they not waste their time and effort. If you stop everything you did to achieve your weight loss, you will quickly end up right back at your starting weight. The mind-set that weight loss is a finite plan that one can start and stop has allowed many to face yearly disappointment as they lose only to regain. This cycle of success and failure creates a toxic relationship with food and exercise that can become very difficult to break once it has begun. Breaking this mental tie allows for a new understanding of how your body functions and how you are a co-creator with God in the remodeling of your physique. If you follow XYZ diet plan you will probably not look like the woman in the ads, but by incorporating healthier practices you can re-create a healthier you.

8

My Body, My Temple, God's Choice

What woman has not looked in the mirror at some point in her life and wanted to change something? If we had to name the top three parts of our bodies we would like to alter, most of us could rattle off the list within seconds. We have spent ample time dissecting our flaws—often more time than we have spent appreciating our assets. We are more likely to see the good in someone else's body than in our own, causing us to pursue the image of the body we want. Body envy is the number one reason women have developed a love-hate relationship with their bodies.

I recall a debate with a friend about whether it was better to be heavy in the chest area or in the hip area. As a curvy hip girl, Christy was adamant that it was impossible to lose her bottom no matter how long she walked on the treadmill or rode on the stationary bike. As a cleavage-enhanced chest girl, I was adamant that it was impossible to drop a bra size without dropping! We both lamented our personal woes over our specific trouble spots while wishing we had the other woman's problem. Years later we have both come to realize that we cannot change our genetics, but we can change our perspective.

Our bodies are part of the nonverbal communication that tells others something about us. When you first meet a person, you make assumptions based primarily on physical findings. Often these initial assumptions stay embedded in our subconscious until we get a chance to really know someone. For this reason, many people have become obsessed with obtaining a body that portrays the image they desire. This first impression is important, but it is only a shallow glance into what constitutes who we are as individuals. Yet the desire to make that first impression perfect has led to a cookie-cutter mentality about what constitutes a healthy body. God has never been one to stay within the confines of our minds. He does not follow molds or patterns when creating individuals. He sees each body as an opportunity to create; however, you provide him with the building material.

My Body

I am responsible for my body. I must supply it with the nutrition it needs to have energy through each day. I must allow it the rest it needs to rejuvenate. I am in charge of pushing it to perform at its optimal level. It is my job to maintain my body so that it will last me the duration of my journey. It is a gift given to me by God; however, unlike most gifts I receive in life, God retains ownership. I am responsible for my body, but I do not own my body. Just because I do not own it does not give me license to abuse it, as abusing it will not only be detrimental to me but also to the One who entrusted me with such a precious gift.

It's amazing how adaptable our bodies are to change. If you consume less than your body needs to maintain its current level of activity, your body will use some of the stored nutrients in your fat and muscle cells to feed itself. Conversely, if you increase your intake, your body will adjust by expanding in places you never knew fat could accumulate. If you exercise muscles they will tighten and increase their capacity to work. The more you work them, the more efficient they become at doing their job. However, if the only exercise your biceps see is applying your mascara, they will slowly shrivel up as your muscle mass diminishes with each passing year. What you do matters. Small investments into our health can have huge dividends. You have the power to improve your health by giving God the building blocks he needs to create a better you.

The foundational building block of health is nutrition. There are no perfect diet plans on the market. Many are excellent starting points to help you learn what changes your body responds to, but ultimately you will need to develop a personal plan that fits your lifestyle. The best approach is to use the food pyramid to begin constructing meal ideas that you enjoy. I can eat a low-carbohydrate, high-protein diet for a few months, but eventually I will crave breads. I can struggle through a few weeks of no desserts before the chocolate dreams awaken me for a midnight ice cream run. Food can become addictive, but I've found that those with even the worst eating disorders can achieve balance when they learn how to eat with a mind-set of freedom.

Diets create a sense of bondage, deprivation, and hope deferred. They leave you wishing you could just be like the thin friend at work who can eat whatever she wants and not gain a pound. The reality is that thin friend you see downing pizza at lunch may be eating only a salad for dinner. The petite woman you saw savoring a Cinnabon at the mall could be rewarding herself for a week of faithfully working out. Every patient I have who has successfully lost weight and kept it off is on an individualized diet plan. Most count calories as a way of keeping track of their intake, but each enjoys those foods they love in moderation and still keeps the weight off.

These weight loss successes are no longer limited in their perceptions of how they must eat to maintain a healthy weight. For these ladies the word *diet* does not bring up images of celery sticks and bland baked chicken, but rather of nutritionally balanced meals they and their families enjoy. For some those meals are primarily take out; for others they are all home-cooked. Regardless of the avenue you take, you can create a personal diet plan that gives you the freedom to enjoy food again without guilt or shame.

I recall having to lose my post-baby weight after my second son. With a twenty-one-month-old and a newborn at home, cooking was not a viable option. Takeout was a meal staple, and I had to figure out how to make it work within a healthy diet plan. My friends and colleagues were amazed that I could lose weight while going to drive-through restaurants most days for dinner. The secret was planning. The computer is an excellent asset for learning the nutritional value of fast food, and I created a list of meals between four hundred and five hundred calories at all of my favorite fast-food restaurants. Paired with a healthy, low-calorie breakfast and lunch, I was able to adjust my diet plan during this stressful time and still lose weight. Freedom has options and it allows you to adapt to any situation.

My Temple

The second building block is exercise. Your body is designed to be in motion. Even when you sleep, parts of your body are actively moving. From the blood within your vessels to the cells transmitting through your brain, there is never a time that you are completely motionless. Exercise can improve many of the health concerns troubling women today. Diabetes, hypertension, obesity-induced arthritis, and high cholesterol levels all respond favorably to movement. Movement provides your body the opportunity to discover what it is capable of doing.

After the birth of my children, I found myself weighing over two hundred pounds and in need of some self-care. I had neglected the gift God had given me, rationalizing that I was too busy to work out and eat better. I soon found out I was too busy not to work out and get myself back on track to a healthier lifestyle. When you are five foot two and over two hundred pounds, it's very difficult to chase a toddler while holding a ten-pound infant. I needed my muscles to cooperate with me and help me not only to keep up with my kids but also to keep up with the demands I was placing on my joints with the extra weight. As much as I hate to admit it, my old office was across the street from the YMCA. You would think that would be enough motivation to stay in shape! So after laying aside all my excuses, I finally joined the gym.

I remember the first day I walked into the gym. Every woman there looked like she had stepped out of a fitness magazine, except for one precious woman who impacted me greatly. Each day we both arrived around the same time. Each day she mounted the treadmill and took off. She was probably over three hundred pounds, but she carried herself with a confidence that had no guilt or shame. She was there with the hundred-and-twenty-pounders, panting on the treadmill right beside them, giving it her all in her shorts and tee. I recall one rainy day when we were the only ones in the gym working out. The rain had held back the typical lunch hour crowd. As she programmed the treadmill, she said, "Making up your mind to do it *is* the battle." That same woman is now over a hundred pounds lighter and has seen how God can use the tools given to create a healthier tomorrow.

A sedentary lifestyle is bondage. It may seem like freedom initially, but ultimately it will lead to increased disease and declining health. Free women move. Embrace the ability to use your body to tone your muscles, to strengthen your heart and lungs, and to improve your flexibility. Regardless of your age or your current physical ailments, there is some level of movement that you can incorporate within your lifestyle. Women who hate formal exercise and gym equipment can turn on their favorite music, close the door, and dance around their living rooms doing the electric slide or the Macarena. The purpose is to move, to be free, to use muscles you do not typically use in your daily activities, to enjoy your body.

God's Choice

The third building block of health is your spiritual well-being. The value you place on yourself will dictate the degree with which you care for your body. Discussing weight loss with a depressed person will only result in further depression. For an anxious woman, trying to find time to work out will only make her more anxious. It is important to find a place of spiritual and mental balance prior to embarking on any healthy changes. Weight loss has its ups and downs. Exercise is not always fun. There must be a stabilizing mind-set that sustains you during the low points. There must be something significant enough that it keeps you on track during your journey to better health, and that something is you. You are worth the effort.

As excited as I was about losing over sixty pounds after my pregnancies, I had a very difficult time enjoying my new body. It was lighter. It was toned. It fit in smaller clothes. All of these were things I wanted and had hoped for, yet I was still not content because it did not look like the bodies I saw in the swimsuit catalog. I was exercising for over an hour five days a week. My calorie count was adequate and well below my needs. Staring with displeasure at the result in the mirror, I wondered where I had failed.

When you do all you know to do and don't get the outcome you hope for, it's easy to fall into a pity party. After the party was over, I was left with the daunting task of cleaning up my mental mess. There were numerous changes that I could have made to my eating plan and workout regimen. There were plenty of places for further improvement, but those changes were beyond what I was willing to do. I didn't want to skip meals to fit into a size 4. I was not willing to increase my time on the elliptical machine to ninety minutes in order to reach a body mass index of 22. I was happy with the level of my current efforts since they had, after all, resulted in a sixty-pound weight loss. Upon further analysis, I realized that I had not failed in my attempt at getting healthy but had failed in my ability to submit to God's sovereignty in every area of my life. I had failed to become a yielded vessel who could accept the outcome of my new healthy lifestyle.

As you supply God the building blocks needed for a healthy change, allow yourself to internalize Jeremiah 18:6, "As the clay is in the potter's hand, so are you in my hand." The reality is that no amount of exercise or dieting will produce a carbon copy of someone else's body. Yes, it is your body, and yes, it is the temple of God's Spirit, but you are not the final decision maker on its appearance. The Master Potter has reserved that privilege. As yielded vessels, we can do our part in preserving the temple and leaving the look of the final product up to him. It is an act of trust and submission. It is a willingness to accept the finished product even if it does not turn out exactly as you planned. Yielding the outcome of your efforts to God will free you to enjoy the positive changes within your body.

Expulsion—*Dynamic Interference Required*

All Scripture is inspired by God and is useful to teach us what is true and to make us realize what is wrong in our lives. It corrects us when we are wrong and teaches us to do what is right. God uses it to prepare and equip his people to do every good work.

2 Timothy 3:16–17

God's Word holds life-changing dynamic power that can intervene in every aspect of your life, even your health. From your diet to your activity level, the Scriptures hold keys that allow a deeper understanding of how God is able to give you a second chance at better health. Provide him the broken pieces of past dieting attempts. Surrender the fragments of poor body image. Allow the warmth of his love to melt the hardened places of your spirit as the Potter molds you into a new vessel.

- God is in control of my life.

In his hand is the life of every creature and the breath of all mankind.

Job 12:10 NIV

- God is able to re-create me.

Therefore, if anyone is in Christ, he is a new creation; the old has gone, the new has come!

2 Corinthians 5:17 NIV

- I am a carrier of God's Spirit.

You surely know that your body is a temple where the Holy Spirit lives. The Spirit is in you and is a gift from God. You are no longer your own. God paid a great price for you. So use your body to honor God.

1 Corinthians 6:19–20 CEV

- God's Spirit brings changes that I cannot control.

Only God's Spirit gives new life. The Spirit is like the wind that blows wherever it wants to. You can hear the wind, but you don't know where it comes from or where it is going.

John 3:8 CEV

- God's Spirit is active and moving, so I should be active and moving.

The earth was barren, with no form of life; it was under a roaring ocean covered with darkness. But the Spirit of God was moving over the water.

Genesis 1:2 CEV

- God is able to feed my mind, my body, and my spirit to satisfaction.

And Jesus said to them, "I am the bread of life. He who comes to Me shall never hunger, and he who believes in Me shall never thirst."

John 6:35 NKJV

- Conventional diets are like the laws that came to condemn and restrict.

The Law came, so that the full power of sin could be seen. Yet where sin was powerful, God's kindness was even more powerful. Sin ruled by means of death. But God's kindness now rules, and God has accepted us because of Jesus Christ our Lord. This means that we will have eternal life.

Romans 5:20–21 CEV

• Christ gives me the freedom to enjoy food.

For why should my freedom be limited by what someone else thinks? If I can thank God for the food and enjoy it, why should I be condemned for eating it?

1 Corinthians 10:29–30

• God has provided an abundance of food, but I need only take what my body requires.

Then the LORD said to Moses, "Look, I'm going to rain down food from heaven for you. Each day the people can go out and pick up as much food as they need for that day. I will test them in this to see whether or not they will follow my instructions."

Exodus 16:4

• Fruits and vegetables are a vital part of God's dietary plan.

Then God said, "Look! I have given you every seed-bearing plant throughout the earth and all the fruit trees for your food."

Genesis 1:29

• I can enjoy my favorite foods in moderation without guilt.

They [hypocrites] will say it is wrong to be married and wrong to eat certain foods. But God created those foods to be eaten with thanks by faithful people who know the truth. Since everything God created is good, we should not reject any of it but receive it with thanks. For we know it is made acceptable by the word of God and prayer.

1 Timothy 4:3–5

- The bread of God's Word is a staple in my spiritual diet.

I am the living bread which came down from heaven. If anyone eats of this bread, he will live forever; and the bread that I shall give is My flesh, which I shall give for the life of the world.

John 6:51 NKJV

- Physical and spiritual exercise prepares me for my future.

Exercise daily in God—no spiritual flabbiness, please! Workouts in the gymnasium are useful, but a disciplined life in God is far more so, making you fit both today and forever.

1 Timothy 4:8–9 Message

- My body is my sacrifice.

And so, dear brothers and sisters, I plead with you to give your bodies to God because of all he has done for you. Let them be a living and holy sacrifice—the kind he will find acceptable.

Romans 12:1

- God is glorified when I make good health choices.

So whether you eat or drink or whatever you do, do it all for the glory of God.

1 Corinthians 10:31 NIV

- My bad health habits show disrespect to God.

Dear friends, we have these promises from God, so we should make ourselves pure—free from anything that makes body or soul unclean. We should try to become holy in the way we live, because we respect God.

2 Corinthians 7:1 NCV

• God wants to help me improve my health.

Trust in the LORD with all your heart; do not depend on your own understanding. Seek his will in all you do, and he will show you which path to take.

Proverbs 3:5–6

• God, the Master Potter, can make me a new vessel.

Then I went down to the potter's house, and behold, he was working at the wheel. And the vessel that he was making from clay was spoiled in the hand of the potter; so he made it over, reworking it into another vessel as it seemed good to the potter to make it.

Jeremiah 18:3–4 AMP

• I am free to enjoy my new body.

We have freedom now, because Christ made us free. So stand strong. Do not change and go back into the slavery of the law.

Galatians 5:1 NCV

Detachment—*Cut the Ties (Snip, Snip)*

Allow the Potter to make you over again. You will be free from past destructive health patterns. Today is a new day. The hand of God can mend food addictions, sedentary habits, smoking, overeating, and emotional eating. Rejoice in the freedom you have to be an active participant in your health. Accept the guidance of God's Spirit as he leads and directs

102

you to healthier options on a daily basis. Being made over requires a level of submission that can be uncomfortable, but the only way to mold clay is for it to be soft and pliable. What type of beautiful vessel does God plan to sculpt you into? The only way to find out is to draw close enough to the Potter for him to see the fractured areas that are in need of his touch.

Balance

9

Life Is an All-or-None Activity

"This is going to hurt," Liz said as the needle pressed into the soft tissue of Jennifer's arm. Finally breaking through the skin's protective layer, Liz skillfully angled the metal intruder around in search of a vein.

Jennifer stared down at her arms. She had rolled up the sleeves of her light blue shirt to give Liz easy access to both sides. From just below her sleeve glared the remnants of her aggressor, a shiny pink scar the size of a quarter. *How could something so small have such a profound effect on my life?* she mused as she recounted the events of the past three months.

⟡⟡⟡

The lack of parking spaces should have been Jennifer's sign to cancel her scheduled appointment, but having wasted the time to get this far she conceded and went inside. As if the parking wasn't bad enough, there was only one seat open in the crowded waiting room.

"Dr. Dalton-Smith had an emergency and is running behind today," the receptionist stated apologetically as Jennifer signed the check-in sheet.

Jennifer slid into the empty seat, thankful to have it as she watched even more cars circling the parking lot. It was 1:30 p.m. and without fail she had to be out of there no later than 3:00 p.m. to pick up her twin teens from school. She flipped open the latest edition of *Good Housekeeping*, a luxury she had not enjoyed in many months. "Mrs. Cassen," called the nurse, just as Jennifer finished typing the ingredients of a delicious-sounding slow-cooker meal into her PDA.

The nurse led her through the back area to an exam room. A gown and a drape were laid out on the exam table, which was right beside an auspicious-looking instrument tray complete with the supplies for her annual exam.

"If you would please put these on, the doctor will be right with you," the nurse instructed, indicating the gown and drape.

The clock in the exam room read 2:40 p.m. She had already been waiting for over an hour and now only had twenty minutes before she had to be on her way to the school. Had it not been for the unexplained fatigue and weight loss she had been experiencing, Jennifer would have walked out of the office. It had been over seven years since her last annual exam, and she had longed for neither her Pap smear nor mammogram in that time. Reluctantly, she pulled on the gown and sat on the exam table as she fanned the paper drape over her exposed legs.

⟨⟩

"I am so sorry I've kept you here so long. Thanks for waiting patiently. It's been a long time since your last exam. You are past due for a complete physical." I smiled as I entered the exam room.

Jennifer's demeanor was pleasant, but it was apparent her wait had understandably caused some irritation. After a round of preliminary questions, I had a general understanding of Jennifer's concerns and a list of recommended screening tests. We proceeded to the physical exam. As I placed the cervical brush specimen in the culture solution, I noticed a small mole on Jennifer's left arm.

"How long have you had that mole on your arm?" I immediately asked.

Jennifer looked down in the direction of my gaze, staring at the small lesion as if seeing it for the first time. "Who's got time to keep up with every little bump?" she jeered, obviously irritated that such an insignificant little spot was prolonging her visit.

I moved her gown aside to get a closer look at the area. The image was worthy of a medical textbook photo shoot. An asymmetric, irregular, discolored, dime-sized, raised lesion grew defiantly on Jennifer's upper arm. A week later the biopsy results confirmed my suspicions: malignant melanoma.

⁂

Two surgeries, a round of radiation therapy, and multiple doctor visits later, Jennifer now found herself in treatment chair #3 on the fourth-floor outpatient oncology ward for her fifth round of chemotherapy.

Time had always been a commodity Jennifer spent on others. Prior to her diagnosis she had always been too busy to do anything for herself. Her life revolved around soccer practices, cheerleading meets, and weekly chores. Friendships had taken a back burner to family obligations. Personal time had become a luxury rather than a necessity.

Now her personal time in room 400 was a necessity. No longer could she ignore her own needs in order to advance those of others. If she wanted to be available to her family in the future, she had to make time to take care of herself. *What if I had walked out of the doctor's office that day?* She contemplated her fate had she decided to leave rather than stay. The oncologist's words echoed daily in her subconscious: "Had this cancer not been found when it was, you would have been dead in a year."

Who would have thought such a tiny mole could cause so much damage? Jennifer had no idea when it had appeared and had not even noticed it until it was pointed out to her during her physical exam. How could something so deadly be growing and multiplying in her body without her knowledge? How could it have invaded her lymphatic system, slowly working its way through every area of her body with no signs and symptoms?

She thought about what she almost lost due to her self-neglect. The faces of her twin girls flashed into view. She was so proud of them. A wave of emotion swelled in her throat as she envisioned what their lives would have been like had the doctor's words proved true. *Dead in one year.* No one to mentor them about how to be a good wife and mother, no mother to help plan future weddings, no mother to stand by their sides as they each gave birth to their first child.

Over the course of her weeks of radiation and chemotherapy, Jennifer learned just how self-sufficient the girls had become. Awakening late one Saturday morning after a particularly draining week of radiation, Jennifer found the girls chopping vegetables in the kitchen.

"What are you two up to?" she questioned.

"We found this super easy Crock-Pot recipe on your computer and thought we'd try to make it for dinner." They smiled. Unbeknownst to them, the twins had stumbled upon the very recipe Jennifer found while waiting for that fateful physical. It was a recipe that took on special meaning for all of them in the months to come.

⌒⊙⌒

Jennifer startled as the needle pricked her yet again, and she suddenly remembered where she was.

"I am so sorry. I don't mean to hurt you," Liz empathized, assuming the tears slipping from Jennifer's eyes were the result of physical pain rather than tears of joy over the blessings in her life.

Liz continued prodding around after rolling veins to no avail. Jennifer rested her head on the reclining chair and closed her eyes, willing the needle and her vein to cooperate. She took a deep breath, remembering the scent from the flowers along the hospital's sidewalk. Two months ago if you had asked her when was the last time she had taken a leisurely walk, she would not have been able to think back that far. Now her routine included a stroll around the hospital's pavilion prior to each treatment. It was her chance to mentally take some of the outside beauty into the bleak white confines of the hospital's interior.

"Gotcha!" Liz smiled as a flash of blood climbed the needle's chamber. She threaded the IV line into Jennifer's yielded vein. Jennifer smiled inwardly, thankful for a second chance at enjoying her life.

Lie #4: Life Is an All-or-None Activity

The all-or-none principle states that either you carry an action through all the way to completion or you don't even attempt it. You either exercise daily or you don't exercise at all. You either read your Bible daily or you don't bother. You either spend quality time with your friends regularly or you stop all communication. You either get your annual physicals done yearly or you omit them. You either spend time nurturing your needs or you neglect them. The all-or-none principle should never become a way of living. Life is not about boundaries but rather about options. The key to effectively utilizing the twenty-four hours we each have in a day is to allow time not only for mundane mandatory activities but also for those things that enrich our lives.

Many women make a conscious daily decision about whether they will carve out some much needed personal time or use that time for more pressing issues, such as the stack of toys piling up on the living room floor. As time progresses, we become set in our patterns of living, choosing to repeat the pattern of the prior day. It's reasonable for a mother who is breast-feeding her newborn to feel limited in her ability to break away for an hour of relaxation. But many moms carry this nursing mentality into their children's teen years, feeling as if their lives must be on hold until their children are finally off to college. Eventually they begin to feel trapped in their lives, bound by the very people they love.

Friends and activities that were once important become secondary, often completely obliterated from the scene. Hobbies and activities that you once enjoyed all of a sudden seem selfish and unnecessary. This mental tie leads to a wrong belief that you cannot simultaneously enjoy the various facets of living, but that you must decide which parts of your life you will keep and which you are willing to sacrifice for now. The problem with this mentality is that it suspends your life to be enjoyed at a later date. It limits your ability to be whole and happy now. No one is promised tomorrow. What happens if tomorrow never comes? What happens is you miss numerous opportunities intended for your enjoyment today.

Illumination—*Peek Inside Yourself*

The major by-products of this mental tie are depression, stress, and fatigue. As these toxic emotions build up in your system, they predispose you to such medical problems as fibromyalgia, chronic fatigue syndrome, and panic attacks. When you omit self-rejuvenation, your emotional battery will begin to run dry, which in turn will cause a negative effect in your physical body. Personal time is necessary for self-discovery and opens the way for a fresh perspective on life. Our times of reconnecting with ourselves lead us back to the basic source of our joy and happiness. It is very difficult to access what you need to be happy if you have not spent time peeking inside yourself. And if you don't know what you need to be happy, you likely will not be successful in finding the wholeness you seek.

Do any of the following statements describe you?

- I feel as if I spend all of my time doing things for my family.
- I am too busy to participate in hobbies and activities I enjoy.
- I feel guilty taking time away from my children to do something special for myself.
- I believe that personal time is a waste of my time.
- It annoys me when friends or family call because I don't have time to talk to them.
- I get stressed when I think about all the things I have to do in a day.
- I feel that I will have more time to live my life once the kids are all grown up.
- I procrastinate on things I know I should be doing for my health and well-being.

- I find it difficult to say no to someone when asked to do something.
- I feel as if there are not enough hours in the day to do all the things I need to do.
- I often feel depressed and overwhelmed by all I have to do.
- I do not enjoy my life as much as I feel I should.
- I feel my life is lacking in joy and laughter.
- I feel emotionally depleted.

A living flow of God's energy is available to fill our joy tanks. Daily times of refreshing allow us to plug into this resource and are the prescription against depression, anxiety, and stress disorders. It is best to consummate this spiritual relationship in solitude rather than in the busy confines of our daily grind. In order to renew our minds, there must be a time of self-nurturing. In addition to the spiritual side, it is also important to incorporate physically and emotionally gratifying activities into our day that give us something to look forward to. This combination produces a balanced level of well-being that is our protection against spiritual, physical, and emotional burnout.

Has your life become too busy for joy? Is there no longer room to just have fun? Does every activity have to have a finite goal for it to be worthwhile? Is there too much noise within your hectic schedule to hear your body's cry for mental rest? When was the last time you penciled in an appointment with yourself?

Activation—*Change Is Hard Work and It May Involve Sweat*

The following activities are trivial for some, but I have found that a large number of my female patients cannot tell me the last time they did one of them. When did you last take a leisurely walk alone to enjoy nature, visit a florist or garden shop to buy yourself a beautiful bouquet, read through a magazine cover to cover just for fun, take a long hot bubble bath, sit in silence to savor a hot cup of tea, enroll in a dance class or art class, park your car in a quiet spot to meditate, or stare at the beauty of the night sky? These are all small ways to begin incorporating a sense of self-nurturing.

It is not necessary to sacrifice self to advance the lives of those you love. On the contrary, it is vital that you nurture yourself in order to be a vibrant, victorious contributor to their lives. The more time you spend building up your internal resources, the more efficient you will become in addressing your family's needs. Investing in your own joy can reap a lifetime of dividends for you and your family. What would happen if you spent five percent of your day doing something just for you? Five percent seems very small, but in actuality it can be a substantial amount of time and make the difference between just being alive and really living.

Let's say in a typical day you awake at 7:00 a.m. You work from 8:00 a.m. to 5:00 p.m. and you go to bed at 11:00 p.m. So there are sixteen hours during your day when you are active. Five percent of your day would be roughly forty-five minutes. If you are also responsible for taking care of the kids and cooking the meals, this may seem like an impossible task. But life is not all or none, and you don't have to set aside this time in one sitting. Even if you only spend five minutes doing something just for you, it will lift your spirits, calm your mind, and bring a sense of joy. Spread that out over four or five ten-minute mental breaks in the course of every day and you will find yourself enjoying more of your life and feeling liberated to share your joy with others.

Take five minutes before you get out of bed to stretch and send up a prayer of gratitude for the new day. Listen to your favorite type of music on your twenty-minute morning commute or even try a new radio station. Spend ten minutes of your lunch hour visiting with a friend by phone or email. To reconnect with your creative side, keep a pad and pencil in your purse to write a poem or sketch while waiting on the kids to finish soccer practice. Do an internet search for some quick meals you can make with your kids and use that time to learn about their day in a non-threatening atmosphere. Play inspirational music while you do household chores to help make even those things you hate more palatable. Take a ten-minute bubble bath or a leisurely steamy shower before bed to unwind tense muscles. Spend ten minutes reading your Bible before lying down to sleep to help quiet your thoughts. It is not necessary for anyone to do all of these in the course of a day, but incorporating any of these activities will rebuild your daily reserve of contentment and rejuvenate your soul.

Transition—*Stretched to the Max but Rebounding with Grace*

Your day should not become so routine that it no longer requires your presence. Nor should your life become a checklist of things that you *must* do and devoid of things you *want* to do. Your personal level of satisfaction directly affects your ability to convey support and love to others. You cannot give what you do not have. Isn't it time to reclaim your lost passions? Recall those things that once brought you pleasure but that you no longer do. What keeps you from participating in those activities? How would being able to do that activity at least once a week or month affect your overall sense of well-being?

There is an opportune time to do things, a right time for everything on the earth (see Ecclesiastes 3). There is a time to work and a time to play. There is a time for family and a time for self. There is a time for laughter and a time for silence. There is a time to hold on and a time to let go. There is a time to tear down old mental ties and a time to build new healthy mind-sets. Could it be that the right time is now?

10

My Balanced Life Requires Addition and Subtraction

It's freezing down here. Where are the lights? Does anyone know I'm here? I don't like this place. I have dirt and debris all around me. Is that manure? It's so dry. I can't recall the last time I had a drink. Every part of me is shriveling up and dying on the inside. I can feel myself hardening from the harsh elements. Whatever is holding me together is slowly slipping away. I don't think I'm going to survive this winter season.

What is this? I feel warmth surrounding me. It's heating me up all the way to the center of my being. This wonderful light is overcoming the dark places. But I'm still so thirsty—if only I could get a drink. Is that thunder I hear in the distance? Yes, rain! This isn't a sprinkling but a deep, penetrating, steady flow. I can feel it engulfing me. I am soaking in this oasis of renewal. My shriveled areas are beginning to smooth. I'm no longer parched as my thirst is satisfied. I feel better, but I still don't like this place. I'm not what I want to be. I'm not happy in this place. I want more.

I feel something pulling at the inside of me. What's going on? This doesn't feel good. It's as if something is threatening to tear me apart from the inside. It's ripping away at my soul. I feel as if it will utterly destroy me if I submit to it. I'm being stretched beyond anything I have known. I'm being asked to go beyond my past limitations. I'm being called to come to a higher level. This call is like a magnet pulling me up. I can feel my old boundaries giving way as I push past my restraints. I push beyond the dirt and debris. I reach up into the heavens to the One calling me. He extends his hands toward me. In his hands are the provisions I need to go further than I've ever gone before.

I take in the nutrients of his grace. I absorb the fertilizer of his love. I digest the flow of his mercy. I can feel myself growing stronger each day. Each day I am lifted higher. New life is blooming all around me. The wind of his Spirit is blowing upon me, spreading my fragrance to all who come along my path. I can feel the light of his glory surrounding me. This is what I was meant to be. I was made to reflect his glory. Oh no, what's happening? I was so beautiful, but now the rain has stopped. I can feel the beginning of the past dryness trying to return. In desperation I quiet my soul. What is that I hear? It is the trickle of a nearby stream. The busy hum of life had prevented my hearing it. How do I get to it for refreshing? I need his help again. I can feel a downward pull as he establishes my roots. He's positioned me to receive this living water. He has sustained me. Daily I will drink deeply from this living river of life.

I have always wondered how a seed must feel. Can you image what it must feel like to be buried alive? There is life on the inside, but the surroundings are not what we would consider pleasant by most standards. However, in the right circumstances God can take what looks dead and breathe life back into it. Like a seed, you have the potential to experience resurrection in the areas of your life that are not producing joy and happiness. But be patient, the journey may include some germination time to allow you to sprout, grow, and develop.

It's a New Season

As I watch the second snowstorm of this winter forming outside, a part of me is anticipating spring's arrival. Spring has always held special significance to me. A part of me loves spring because it occurs during my birthday month. But more than that, spring has always represented new life. The first blades of grass begin to arise out of what appears to be dead ground. Bulbs, whose stems have long ago withered, shoot up new sprouts as a promise of things to come. Buds of life clothe trees that have been bare for months. Spring cleaning brings out mops and brooms to rejuvenate homes. Yard sales begin to appear on every corner, and old objects that have lost their use in one home become the next owner's newfound treasures. Winter clothes get boxed up and placed aside as we revitalize lighter garments to serve our needs. The promise of Easter Sunday overcomes the solemn implication of Good Friday. Everything concerning spring is a testimony of resurrection life.

What is it about spring that makes us want to slam the door shut on winter as soon as possible? Spring brings the promise of hope. Hope is rooted in faith. Each spring is an exercise in faith that those things around us that look dead can return to life. If God can bring a plant back to life that has been frozen by harsh elements, deprived of nutrients, covered by debris, and hidden from the sun, how much more can he renew the dead places of our lives? When we make room in our homes by getting rid of things that have lost their value to us, we make room for new things that bring us joy. In the same way that you box up last year's sweaters to make room for spring's Bermuda shorts, you can mentally box up last year's failures and make room for this year's opportunities.

There are seasons of life. Everyone will experience the seasons of winter, spring, summer, and fall. Some phases of life will be harder to deal with than others. Through spring, summer, and fall seasons there is still more good than bad; however, in the winter season it appears as if everything has died. Most of us have difficulty finding our way out of winter into spring. You may be in a winter season now. It may be a hundred degrees outside, but spiritually your winter season can come at any month of the year and at any age of your life.

It is not hard to determine whether you are in a winter season. You are in a winter season if you are depressed. You are in a winter season if you are discontent with your life. You are in a winter season if you have difficulty smiling or laughing. You are in a winter season if you are anxious and fretful. You are in a winter season if you have become emotionally hard and dry. You are in a winter season if you have lost hope. You are in a winter season if doubt has overcome faith. You are in a winter season if you can no longer feel the warmth of God's love. You are in a winter season if you feel buried under the weight of your problems and concerns.

Winter is only for a season. How long your winter season lasts is in part up to you. The key difference between winter and spring is light. Cloudy days devoid of the sun's warmth characterize winter. The entrance of spring brings with it not only the clearing of the clouds but the light and heat of the sun. This light penetrates past the surface to the deep hidden areas. This warmth awakens seeds of hope, seeds of life, and seeds of joy. As they seek more of the light, these seeds push aside fear, doubt, anger, grief, hope deferred, and depression. The duration of your winter seasons depends upon how quickly you get yourself in the right place to receive the light of God's love for you. His light will usher you into your new season.

Private Garden

> You are my private garden, my treasure, my bride, a secluded spring, a hidden fountain.
>
> Song of Solomon 4:12

When God looks at you he sees a beautiful array of emotions, characteristics, and traits that combine to form a private garden into which he desires entry. It is here that contentment, joy, and peace can be cultivated. The garden of your soul is where your life is either nurtured into a bountiful harvest or neglected to the point of decay. Any good gardener will attest to the need for balance. If you give plants too much water, molds may form. If you give too much sunshine, dryness can overcome the plants. If you do not provide adequate fertilizer, the plant will not grow to its maximum potential. If weeds are not removed, they will overtake the entire garden. In the same way, there are weeds that attempt to take over our personal lives. Weeds of stress and pressure can easily become the prominent fruit being produced from our day-to-day interactions. Instead of enjoying the fragrance of a balanced life, we are left with the disgusting smell of wasted time.

> Blow on my garden and spread its fragrance all around. Come into your garden, my love; taste its finest fruits.
>
> Song of Solomon 4:16

Allow God into your private garden. Invite him to breathe new insights into those areas of your life you need decreased in order to make room for those things that are most important to you. Too often I meet patients in their senior years who voice feelings that they have missed out on life. They share regrets over time spent doing things in preparation for the future while missing the joy of living in the moment. They bemoan disappointment over lost opportunities and relationships that they didn't maintain. My comment to them is always the same: "What's stopping you now?" You can rectify whatever you feel you are missing out on if you are willing to embrace change. When God blows on your garden he may bend some stems, sway some leaves, and blow off some petals. There will be some changes in how your garden appears, but the fragrance released will be worth it.

An Aerial View

Take a moment to look at your life from a higher perspective. Imagine your life as a garden spread out over a large field. The different aspects of your life are planted in groups within the field. There are specific places for family, career, finances, health and fitness, recreation, personal development, friends, marriage and romance, and spirituality. Now what does the layout of your life look like? If you were to fly above your field, which areas would have the most productivity and which areas would be barren? Is there an abundance of finances but a lack in family? Has family weeded out romance? Is fruit arising from the spirituality field?

It would be impossible to spread your life equally around all of these different areas. The stress of trying to be everything to everyone would lead to an unhappy life and an early death. The goal is to assess how your field looks and to make

121

sure you are seeding those areas that are important to you. Every field will look different. There are no right or wrong percentages of growth in each field. You alone know what parts of your garden bring you the greatest joy. There will be times when work and family life conflict, but if you know which takes precedence for you it will be easier to make a decision that you are happy with.

It is important to prioritize the areas of your garden. Just because one area has high priority does not mean that you have to spend most of your day focusing on that one thing. It does mean that, from an aerial perspective, that area of your garden should become the most developed and nurtured over time. The key is cumulative time spent in that area. Conversely, neglecting an area that is at the bottom of your priority list will ultimately leave a bare spot that predators can invade. You should visit even those areas from time to time to close the door on outside attacks.

Balance

How would you define the quality of your life today? Do words like *peaceful*, *joyful*, *blessed*, and *satisfied* come to mind? Or do you identify more with words like *discontent*, *ungratified*, and *frustrated*? If the former describes you, then you have successfully found balance within your life. If, however, you identify more with the latter, today is a great day to begin adding to and subtracting from your equation.

Balance is a feeling of emotional, physical, and spiritual harmony. It's a steady state where all components of your life are working together for a common goal: your well-being. When one area is not cooperating, it can cause friction within the system and produce stress. This stress puts pressure on the system and begins to pull at the weak points. Procrastination over improving a known weak spot only leads to increased stress. Neglected health, fractured relationships, and downcast spirits can quickly succumb to stress, which leads to further imbalance within the system. The purpose of balance is to keep the peace by stabilizing the weak spots. You are as strong as the weakest component of your life. You can be financially wealthy, but poor health will sideline your enjoyment of your finances. You can have a thriving career with kids you barely know. It is very easy to get out of balance.

Balance will require addition and subtraction. If you feel out of balance, look again at the aerial view of your life and compare it to your priorities. Often the weak spot that is out of balance *is* one of your priorities, which is why the system is grinding to a halt. You cannot progress toward contentment until you make some adjustments. Begin by simplifying your life. Look over your schedule to see if you have committed your time to areas that are not productive for you. Yes, that charity may be a worthy cause, but if you are participating out of obligation and not from a place of peace you likely are not contributing your best. It would be better to open that volunteer spot up for someone whose heart is in it. It's difficult to obtain fulfillment and joy in situations where our minds have become detached from the activity of the moment. If I'm worried about my kids the whole time I am at work, I will miss my opportunity for career contentment. We have become so skilled at multitasking that life has become a multitask event where our hands and hearts have learned to work independently of each other.

Many women struggle with balance because we get caught in the mental trap that it's all or none. You have to choose either your kids or your career. You have to be either a fitness guru or a couch potato. If your aerial view shows you that you need more time with your kids, you don't have to go to the extreme of quitting your job. Often changing how you spend your time together will strengthen that weak spot and bring the system back into harmony.

I work long hours and have two small children. I enjoy my job and could not imagine giving it up, but my kids are one of my top priorities. I balance the two by incorporating "mommy days" when I plan something fun just for the three of us to do: a day at the arcades, going to a movie, building with Legos, feeding ducks, or whatever reasonable request they conjure up that allows me to be in the moment with them. They love to see me arrive early to pick them up from day care for our adventures. It gives us time to reconnect and gives me time to do things with them I may otherwise miss the chance to do at this age.

One area, however, that I am quick to neglect is that of friends. I have learned that I can easily remedy this by using email and online social networks like Facebook. Both keep me connected with friends without the added pressure of having to plan times for phone calls and dinners. How you balance these areas may look completely different, but the result should be the same. The scale on which you add and subtract will need to reach an equalizing point where your days are spent delighting in your life.

Expulsion—*Dynamic Interference Required*

The Word of God is like seeds that can be sown into your life. These seeds contain the potential to blossom into new hope, renewed joy, and a peace that passes all understanding. However, these seeds can easily be consumed before they have time to take root. Those things that bog down your life, leaving you mentally fatigued and unsatisfied, are like weeds taking over the fertile ground of your mind. Before reading

God's Word, spend a few moments cultivating the land. Remove rocks of unforgiveness, pull up weeds of anxiety, and plow through the hard soil of anger. Prepare your heart and mind to receive the seeds of promise in his Word. Allow his love to shine upon you. Allow his peace to flood you wherever you are each day.

- Growth requires seeds.

The seed is the word of God.

Luke 8:10 NKJV

- The right soil can produce exponential growth.

The seed that fell on good soil represents those who truly hear and understand God's word and produce a harvest of thirty, sixty, or even a hundred times as much as had been planted!

Matthew 13:23

- The glory of God illuminates my path.

The LORD is God, and he has made his light shine upon us.

Psalm 118:27 NIV

- God can transform the dry places in my life.

For the LORD will comfort Zion, He will comfort all her waste places; He will make her wilderness like Eden, and her desert like the garden of the LORD; Joy and gladness will be found in it, thanksgiving and the voice of melody.

Isaiah 51:3 NKJV

- The refreshing water of his love is ever-flowing over me.

The LORD will guide you continually, giving you water when you are dry and restoring your strength. You will be like a well-watered garden, like an ever-flowing spring.

Isaiah 58:11

• Daily I can drink from his streams.

As a deer gets thirsty for streams of water, I truly am thirsty for you, my God. In my heart, I am thirsty for you, the living God.

Psalm 42:1–2 CEV

• Staying connected to God increases my productivity.

Remain in me, and I will remain in you. For a branch cannot produce fruit if it is severed from the vine, and you cannot be fruitful unless you remain in me. Yes, I am the vine; you are the branches. Those who remain in me, and I in them, will produce much fruit. For apart from me you can do nothing.

John 15:4–5

• My choices affect my well-being and balance.

My life constantly hangs in the balance, but I will not stop obeying your instructions.

Psalm 119:109

• God is beckoning me to bloom where I am planted.

Look, the winter is past, and the rains are over and gone. The flowers are springing up, the season of singing birds has come, and the cooing of turtledoves fills the air. The fig trees are forming young fruit, and the fragrant grapevines are blossoming. Rise up, my darling! Come away with me, my fair one!

Song of Solomon 2:11–13

• My soil can produce a harvest of praise.

For as the soil makes the sprout come up and a garden causes seeds to grow, so the Sovereign LORD will make righteousness and praise spring up before all nations.

Isaiah 61:11 NIV

• Praise is the offering of my fertile ground.

Bring the best of the firstfruits of your soil to the house of the LORD your God.

Exodus 23:19 NIV

• My life will celebrate God's goodness.

"He brought us to this place and gave us this land flowing with milk and honey! And now, O LORD, I have brought you the first portion of the harvest you have given me from the ground." Then place the produce before the LORD your God, and bow to the ground in worship before him. Afterward you may go and celebrate because of all the good things the LORD your God has given to you and your household.

Deuteronomy 26:9–11

Detachment—*Cut the Ties (Snip, Snip)*

God wants you to enter your place of balance and well-being. He wants your life watered, fed, and fertilized to the point of producing an abundant harvest of blessings. Your personal fields have the potential to blossom beyond your expectations.

127

The more time spent cultivating the soil, the better the outcome. As you process this mental ground, don't forget to take some time to enjoy the fruit being produced. "How is the soil? Is it fertile or poor? Are there trees on it or not? Do your best to bring back some of the fruit of the land" (Num. 13:20 NIV).

LIE #5

Control

11

Being in Control Is Better Than Spontaneity

"What is your assessment of the damage?" Brenda probed as she pushed the microphone closer to the unsuspecting firefighter who only moments before had barely escaped the flames of an apartment fire.

Sipping her second cup of coffee, she watched the footage as bits and pieces of her interview were skillfully selected for today's morning news broadcast. Brenda's fiery red hair and edgy personality rivaled the electrical charge coming from the wall of viewing screens in the editing room. Most mornings she brought in muffins for the staff, but today the bakery was out. A part of her was miffed over their inability to meet the supply and demand. From her vantage point she could see Jeff, the senior producer, heading toward the room and anticipating his daily bran muffin.

"Hey Brenda, we've just gotten an unbelievable offer to cover an exclusive VIP event in St. Croix. The agent who notified me said it's so big that he can't divulge the involved parties for fear it will leak into the media. He's giving us the rights to exclusively cover the event. The only hitch is that we must have a reporter out there by six this evening, and I want you for this job."

Brenda's line of work was predictably unpredictable, but never had her employer asked her to do something as unusual as fly off to cover some unknown event. As a local news reporter, she liked keeping things within the comfortable confines of her surrounding area. She strived to maintain some level of control over the vicissitudes of life. Whether in her job or in her daily activities, Brenda managed the hours in her day better than most people manage the dollars in their bank accounts. And nowhere in this day had she allowed for time to fly off on some wild adventure to cover someone's island shindig.

"I'm sorry, Jeff, but you're going to have to find someone else to do it. I'm backed up here, and I don't have a thing to wear to something like that."

"Not another word, Brenda. I won't take no for an answer. Take the rest of the day off to get your things packed. I've reserved your flight and a room at the same resort." Jeff's stern expression didn't waver as he passed her the flight and hotel information. "A car will pick you up at the airport," he offered as he walked out the door, leaving no room for compromise.

Brenda could feel the blood rising to her face as a deep flush stained her cheeks. She grabbed her purse and pushed through the front door toward her parked car. Most of the junior reporters would kill over an opportunity for an all-expenses-paid island weekend. She, however, would rather be downtown getting the oil changed in her car like she had been planning to do today at lunch. Change was not an acquaintance Brenda had visited lately. Spontaneity was a threat to avoid, and she had no desire to become its victim today.

Mentally she scrambled for any excuse she could use to get out of going, but she came up empty. Anxiety began to slowly climb as Brenda flipped through her date book looking for a way out. She noticed a name that usually brought a smile to her face, but today his name was yet another reason she didn't want to go. *What if he calls to ask me out on a date this weekend?* They had been dating over the past year, and she still couldn't believe she was fortunate enough to be sought after by one of the most eligible bachelors in town.

She entered her home and ran straight to the closet. Pulling out a notepad, she began jotting down things she would need. "This is ridiculous," she thought out loud. "I don't even know what to pack for something like this. Is it formal, semiformal, or what?"

Mounting anxiety gave way to confusion as she grappled with various outfits in vain, unable to coordinate on the spur of the moment. Having meticulously planned her on-screen outfits months in advance, Brenda had no experience with impromptu packing. She pulled out her cell phone to call her assistant for help. Brenda's assistant had been with her on numerous shoots and had even filled in for her in the past when she was ill. Brenda knew that the two of them would be able to piece together an acceptable solution.

***

The warm breeze from the ocean wafted over the tables covered with white linen. A canopy of yellow, pink, orange, and red splayed across the center of each, leaving a light floral scent in the air. Waiters were busy completing the final preparations for the night's event. The guest list was an exclusive compilation of twenty friends and family handpicked by the host, each flown out for the special event. The quiet bungalow off the island of St. Croix had been reserved for the entire weekend.

The festive atmosphere on the beachside deck was contagious, with each guest eagerly awaiting the arrival of the guest of honor. Participants danced, mingled, and munched their way through the night. From the balcony window, Allen could see the limo pulling up to the bungalow. His smile broadened as he anticipated the look on Brenda's face when she realized she was not here for work but rather for a surprise marriage proposal.

As the chauffeur pulled the last bag out of the car, Allen wondered when Brenda had found time to purchase new luggage. Just as he completed the thought, he watched Brenda's assistant Susan step out of the car.

Lie #5: Being in Control Is Better Than Spontaneity

There are areas of life where control is an appropriate response. We need to control our tempers. We need to gain control over our tongues and the words we speak to others. It's even admirable to have a system that allows you to keep your weight under control. Yet too often we take control to the extreme and try to apply it to every area of our lives. Datebooks and personal data assistants are packed with schedules controlled down to the minute. Our to-do lists are so organized they leave little room for change, spontaneity, or freedom. From the time it takes the mechanic to finish our car to the inventory at the local grocery store, we have expectations of what will happen and how long it will take to get it done. If one or the other fails to live up to our expectations, we begin to feel a lack of control. Unfortunately, it's a misguided feeling because we never actually had control in the first place.

Control requires a regulatory position over something. If you control your diet, you regulate and dictate what is acceptable and what is unacceptable. Similarly, when you try to control every moment of your schedule you become the dominating influence over the events of your day. You become the authoritative figure in your life. The reality is that no one has complete control over her own life. So no matter how hard a person tries to maintain control, it will continue to slip through human fingers. Hands big enough to restrain, direct, and manage all time and events are the only ones that can grasp control. I know only one entity who is capable of such power.

Control is the enemy of freedom. Those who live with the image of being in control have a difficult time embracing freedom. Freedom and control cannot be active at the same time. You cannot be free to speak whatever you want if you are controlling your tongue. You cannot be free to enjoy whatever is at the buffet table if you are controlling your diet. You cannot be free to enjoy the banquet of adventures God has in store for you if you are trying to control every moment of your day. Once you determine that you want to have freedom in an area, you must relinquish control.

Freedom does not look the same for every woman nor does it imply the same thing for everyone. For some women, calling in to work for a day off may be no big deal. But for someone who has a hard time doing things for herself, taking a day off to pamper herself may provide the boost of freedom needed to propel her from self-neglect to self-love. Freedom for you may be trying a new art or dance class. It may be parasailing next time you visit the beach. It could be going back to school for a degree you've always wanted. It may be as simple as leaving an hour open in your date book for you to do nothing. However you define freedom, one element that is consistent is its lack of restraint.

Freedom brings a feeling of liberation. There is a sense of release as you expand and stretch beyond your past limitations. Doors to new opportunities begin to open as the keys of freedom release you. There is an ease of movement that allows for greater exploration in your life. Freedom allows you to recognize your right to enjoy life in its entirety. It's your ticket into the greatest amusement park on earth, full of surprise, joy, and excitement. You never know what new venture awaits.

It's all right letting yourself go, as long as you can get yourself back.

Mick Jagger

Most of us love the elation that spontaneity brings, but, as the above quote from Mick Jagger implies, what would happen if you were unable to regain control after your time of freedom? This fear of the unknown is the basis for the fifth lie. Rather than risk an unknown event, we cling to what miniscule bit of control we are able to place upon our day. For example, a patient once told me she loves walking at the park but never goes at her lunch break because she is always afraid something will happen and she would not be able to get back to work on time. Another patient passed up an opportunity to go to Hawaii because she feared someone would bomb the plane. Both are legitimate concerns, but the only way these two ladies can control these events is by avoidance. Why avoid an opportunity to do something that would bring joy to your life in an attempt to keep some level of control?

Control is ultimately a trade-off between joy and a sense of safety. Rather than allowing yourself to take a chance with joy, you choose the safety of control. But how safe is control? It is only as safe as the one wielding the power. If you must maintain the reins to keep it all in check, then there is no safety at all. At some point in our search for security we have to make a decision about whether God is trustworthy.

Allow your trust in God's goodness, grace, and mercy to become the safety net you depend on in times of uncertainty. The employer at the job you traded your life for could lay you off tomorrow, but when you trust in God's goodness you can anticipate the surprise of an even better opportunity. The slow driver who makes you late for work may just be divine intervention protecting you from an accident that would have occurred had you sped along at your usual pace. Could it be that God is big enough to see the end from the beginning? Now that is real control! Isn't it time we relinquish any pretense of control and accept the spontaneity of freedom by his grace?

Illumination—*Peek Inside Yourself*

Wanting to feel a sense of safety and security in a world so full of uncertainty is completely understandable. We all desire the peace that safety brings with it, but trying to be the provider of that safety is counterproductive. If we were capable of obtaining full disclosure over every aspect of our day, life would lose the very elements that make it interesting.

Do any of the following statements describe you?

- I am good at scheduling my day and put a high value on punctuality.
- I make lists about multiple areas of my life.
- I prefer to do things myself because then I know they will be done right.
- I don't like working in groups or situations where I have to compromise my desires.

- I would not enjoy having someone throw me a surprise party.
- My vacations are planned well in advance with structured activity and little down time.
- I have a hard time enjoying a new outfit or hairstyle the first few times I wear it.
- I get very upset waiting for people who are late or who fail to complete a project at a stated time.
- I prefer to have the remote control when watching television with others.
- I offer others my opinion even when it's not requested.
- I am occasionally accused of sticking my nose into things that are none of my business.
- I feel that my way of doing things is often better than the way others do it.
- If things do not go my way in a situation, I complain and let everyone know.
- If I volunteer for a club, I prefer to be on the organizational committee.

For someone affected by this mental tie, control is far superior to an unexpected surprise—even a good surprise. If you only feel comfortable in situations that you can control, you greatly limit your opportunities for blessings. What has being in control cost you?

Activation—*Change Is Hard Work and It May Involve Sweat*

Brenda arrived at my office one month after missing her own proposal party. Years of living under the pressure of her schedule had caused high blood pressure, and this was her regularly scheduled hypertension checkup.

"Whoa! What's going on with your blood pressure? It hasn't been this high in years," I exclaimed as I flipped through her chart.

Brenda shook her head from side to side as if unsure where to begin. "It's been a rough month." She began pointing to the beautiful new engagement ring on her hand.

"Congratulations, Brenda! That's fantastic news, but from your blood pressure I'm guessing very stressful as well."

Brenda stared down at the ring, twirling it around her finger. She did not respond to my question, which was very atypical for my usually boisterous, over-the-top patient. The silence in the room slowly performed its own surgery as emotions came to the surface for closer examination. Completely unaware of the events of a month ago, I contemplated the possible problems in my mind before proceeding. *Why would a newly engaged woman be so upset?*

"Do you want to marry him? Do you love him?" I probed.

Brenda sat upright in her chair. She smiled at me and laughed at how far off the mark I was. It was good to see some glimmer of her typical personality.

"Dr. Dalton-Smith, I definitely want to marry him. He is the best thing that has ever happened in my life." The smile on her face quickly flattened as she continued. "The problem is that I almost missed my opportunity to be with him."

Brenda went on to explain the events of that day down to the actual proposal, which ended up occurring by phone rather than in person.

"Oh Brenda, I'm so sorry," I said in sympathy. "It sounds like it was going to be a very special moment. What made you do the last-minute switch with your assistant?"

"I had plans for that day and didn't want to change my schedule," she rationalized.

"Was there anything on your schedule that couldn't have waited? Was there anything so important that it couldn't be rescheduled for what sounded like a great opportunity even without knowing about the proposal?"

Brenda shrugged, unable to think of any aspect of that day that was a worthy replacement for what she had missed.

I probed. "Maybe a better question would be, what were you afraid of missing if you left?"

Brenda's eyes blazed a line in my direction. Fear was not an emotion she attached to herself, and the implication that she feared anything had crossed the line. "I wasn't afraid of anything," she retorted.

"Look, Dr. Dalton-Smith, I'm not here to be psychoanalyzed," she stated matter-of-factly as she looked down at her watch. "I just need my blood pressure pills adjusted. If you could please get on with the exam, I have things I need to do."

Feeling the cool breeze as the door to her emotions swung shut in front of me, I motioned for her to sit on the exam table. I proceeded with the perfunctory aspect of her physical exam. The rustling sound of the paper on the exam table was the only noise in the room. Brenda's heart rate was over 110, a telling sign of how upset she had become from my question. She tried hard to maintain even breaths, but her respirations came in short bursts consistent with the survival mode her emotions had entered. I was certain if I had checked Brenda's blood pressure now it would be off the charts.

"All right, Brenda, we're all done. I apologize if I upset you, but I'm concerned about your blood pressure. It's definitely too high and will need additional treatment. I'll be right back with the samples of your new medication."

I walked across the hall to the sample closet, thankful for the reprieve. Before returning to Brenda's room, I stopped by my office for something I thought would help her. As my hand gripped the knob to her room, I sent up a prayer for help.

Brenda was now pacing the room. This was no longer a casual visit. Our uprightness carried the undertones of a confrontation. I had known Brenda for years and knew that this was not her. The loss of that special moment, the guilt of disappointing her fiancé and family that night, and the regret from missing an opportunity that could not be reclaimed had led Brenda into a grieving period that was robbing her of the ability to enjoy her engagement. Anger and depression are a normal part of the grieving process right before the upward turn toward hope, and I was hopeful that Brenda was ready for that transition.

"Okay, I've got your samples here." I smiled. Brenda took the small bag from my hand and walked past me toward the checkout room. While waiting for her turn with the clerk, Brenda reached into her bag to look at the new prescription and felt something. Peeking in, she noticed a card. She pulled it out to read the front of the card: *With deepest sympathy.* Puzzled, she opened the card to read the following:

> Please accept my condolences over your loss. Life has a way of being unpredictable. Although you cannot get back the time that was lost, it would be a shame to lose even more. Despite the disappointment of the proposal, you still ended up with the man of your dreams. Enjoy the current opportunity before it too becomes a source of grief and pain. I'm here if you need to talk.
>
> Dr. Dalton-Smith

Transition—*Stretched to the Max but Rebounding with Grace*

Rather than shopping for dresses, planning venues, tasting cake samples, and coordinating colors, Brenda had spent the past month reliving that missed opportunity. Reliving the one time when trying to maintain control had cost her something big. Grieving over the potentially wonderful memories that were now lost in a sea of what-ifs.

Trying to control life will cost you something. For some the price is peace, for others it's joy, and for still others it's a lost experience. Why pay for something you will never possess? Control is not up for sale; God has reserved the deed in his name. Use the commodity of your time to cash in on all God has in store for you. Live life to the fullest, unbound by fear and rebounding in his grace. The "now" moments of your life are secure in his plan. Receive the safety of his love and embrace the spontaneity of life. You never know what surprise God has in store for you next.

12

Spontaneity Is God's Opportunity to Surprise Me

What is this? I reach out to grasp the box set before me. Excitement and fear simultaneously hold me in their grip. Tentatively I peek inside. The dim light of my emotions limits my vision. With eager anticipation, I take hold of this new phenomenon. Inside is a garment handpicked by God. Its peculiar pattern creates an unusual cascade of light against the backdrop of my life. I would have preferred pleasant pastels rather than these vibrant, fiery tones. This will never blend in with my favorite color scheme. This is definitely not something I would have picked out for myself. Oh, and the fabric—why would he have picked such a horrible texture? This is too rough against the soft skin of my dreams to be comfortable. A smooth transition of satin or silk would have been a more desirable choice. I briefly pull it near for closer inspection. Its abrasive quality rubs at my flesh, causing a place of irritation. I do not like this surprise.

As I recoil from this undesired gift, I stumble and land on my knees. From my kneeling position, a gem from my past becomes visible under a layer of dust. Why had I discarded this one-time treasure and stuffed it into the attic of my life? Look at how it has aged from lack of use. What a shame. If only I could return it to its former beauty. Sitting in a place of regret, disappointment emerges, followed by heartache. An avalanche of current pain floods my good memories. As I arise from my low position, the brilliant array of colors beaming up from the garment draws my attention again.

I reach for this gift that had caused me to run in retreat. I lay my once undesired present upon my lost treasure from the past. Before my eyes the two intertwine and become one new creation. My new surprise becomes the tool through which life is breathed back into my forgotten jewel of the past. The texture is just rough enough to smooth the sharp edges of past failures. The colors are bright enough to overcome every dark moment. There is a restoration of purpose. Everything I despised about the gift has worked out for my good. I cringe at how close I came to tossing this unexpected surprise aside just because I did not like its presentation. Next time I will receive the present with open arms.

Surprise!

Do surprises make you squeal or squirm? Good surprises are always a delight, but unfortunately some surprises are so unexpected that you can feel unprepared and caught completely off guard. Sometimes the surprise may not look like you expected. Sometimes it comes wrapped in layers that you must dissect in order to find the full revelation of its worth. Sometimes it comes when you feel unworthy of receiving the gift. Surprises are not always a welcome occurrence, but they are a part of life.

Surprises by definition should create a sense of wonder and amazement. There should be an awe factor associated with them. They should be abrupt and sudden. If you can anticipate it, then it is not really a surprise. Surprises should come when you least expect them. They should overwhelm your emotions and take your breath away. Let's be honest, surprises can be downright scary at times! Mentally preparing yourself to receive surprises from God opens you to receive blessing after blessing. God's surprises may not always look like what you would have chosen for yourself, but he is the ultimate gift-giver and knows your needs even before you ask.

God's Timing

You may recall numerous times you have prayed and asked God to do something, only to wait and wait and wait. Many months, and in some cases years, may have elapsed with no sign of God's considering your request. It's difficult to keep a spirit of faith alive when it feels like God is not listening. Then one day, when you have given up asking, when you have maybe even laid that dream to rest, God suddenly acts on your behalf. There were no warnings that he would do it, no prelude to the event. But for reasons you will never know, the divine moment arrived when God decided to answer your request.

We all have in mind the day we would like certain blessings to appear. I can recall planning the year I would get pregnant with my first son when I was in medical residency. It could not be that year because I was starting a new job, but the next year would be perfect. Well, God's plan was for Tristan to be born two years later than my plan. Those were the longest two years of waiting in my life. I had come to the conclusion I was not supposed to have kids and had found a sense of peace when suddenly I found out I was pregnant.

We each have our expectations of when we would like to see God do the things we have asked of him, but God also has a day he has purposed for those events. He does not tell us when that day will be, nor does he give us any indication how long we will have to wait. All we can do during these moments is to take a stand of faith that God loves us and is working all things out for our good, even during the times when it seems as if he has said no to our requests. Sometimes it's not really a "no" but a "not right now, be patient and wait on my timing."

God is not limited by times or dates. With him one day is like a thousand years and a thousand years are like one day (see 2 Peter 3:8). We often get so accustomed to waiting on God that we forget God can act suddenly. Learning how to wait with eager anticipation allows you to open your mind to the possibility of having a "suddenly" moment. Your anticipation of seeing God move is your proclamation that with God all things are possible.

The Suddenly Moments of God

The suddenly moments of God are always dramatic and exciting. It's impossible to predict them, and the surprise element makes them hard to dissect. Wouldn't it be great to be able to compile a specific formula for manifesting the suddenly moments of God? Your checkbook is running out of funds before you've paid all the bills and suddenly a check arrives in the mail. Your child is fighting off illness and suddenly is healed overnight. Your mind is overcome with depression when suddenly you receive an abundance of joy and peace.

These types of suddenly moments are fascinating, but what about those moments that are so unexpected that you didn't even know to ask for them? Suddenly God promotes you to a new position that never existed in your company. Suddenly you are pregnant with your fourth child while on birth control pills. Suddenly a major recording artist is pursuing that little song you wrote for your daughter's wedding.

In both types of suddenly moments, God takes full control of the situation and alters the outcome in a dramatic fashion. Whether fervent prayer has hastened the moment or a sovereign God has ordained it, the outcome is an instantaneous turn of events. These moments of sudden intervention have the power to change your view of God. When you invite God's suddenly moments into your life, you create an atmosphere for the miraculous. You set the stage for an extravagant God to do extraordinary things within your life.

Interruptions

God wants to interrupt your life. Imagine going along through your work day doing your usual duties. Your morning coffee has awakened your bladder, so you rush off to the ladies' room. Suddenly you hear sobs coming from under a closed stall door where a co-worker is alone and very upset. God has interrupted your day with the opportunity to console someone in pain.

Let's think of another scenario. You are in the checkout line at the grocery store when suddenly it comes to a standstill. A young mother is at the head of the line frantically scavenging through her purse. You hear the cashier state that she still needs ten dollars to pay her total or put back some of the items. The cart only contains a few items, most of which are baby food and formula. The infant in the cart starts to whine, and you can see the distress on the young mother's face. God has interrupted your shopping trip with someone in need of financial assistance.

Interruptions are a part of suddenly moments. Some interruptions, such as the examples above, can be a part of God's plan for your growth and spiritual maturity. Some interruptions are intended to bless you with gifts from God. Some interruptions are meant to reveal the magnitude of God's power in your life. During these moments, God suddenly intervenes in an unusual, unexplainable, unexpected way that causes you to adjust to his plans. The sudden interruptions of God are part of the great adventure of having a relationship with him. How you handle those interruptions affects the number of opportunities God has to surprise you. Allow yourself to be flexible enough to adjust your plans to accommodate his plans. Aligning with his timing always results in a better ending.

Spontaneity

God is a God of spontaneity. Spontaneity is freedom from constraint. It is the liberty to proceed without formality or rituals. It is the ability to release what you have planned in exchange for what he has for you.

Spontaneity takes faith. Without faith it is impossible to let go of your preconceived ideas. Without faith it is impossible to set aside your specific desires for an unknown adventure. Faith allows you to cling to the idea that God is for you and not against you. It allows you to accept him at his word when he promises that he has a good plan for your life. It allows you to receive a blessing even if you did not go through the formality of specifically praying for it. It releases you to step into favor and abundance at all times, not just when you have completed a specific religious ritual. Faith believes that God wants to bless you and is daily looking for opportunities to bring good into your life.

Spontaneity is like a courtship where you allow God to lavish his goodness upon you. You open the door to his affection and accept the bouquet of his love. You entertain the flow of his grace and partake of the sweetness of his mercy. You invite in the purification of his Spirit and dine within the parameters of his holiness. You dance in tune with the movement of his presence. You become his bride, his beloved, as he finds you open to receive the sudden manifestations of his blessings upon your life.

Expulsion—*Dynamic Interference Required*

The word *suddenly* appears more than one hundred times in the New Living Translation of the Bible. There are many examples of times when God suddenly intervened or interrupted the course of events in the lives of those who trusted in him. He still is the God of suddenly moments, and he desires the freedom to act spontaneously within your life. His timing is perfect, while our skewed perspective of time flaws our timing. Our limited view of the present does not begin to compare with his unlimited view of the past, present, and future. Suddenly moments appear to happen abruptly within our lives, but they are gifts God has planned for a specific time to surprise us with his goodness. We must possess the freedom to accept these suddenly moments for the gifts they are.

There are times when God looks down into our finite lives and sends infinite answers to our needs. Sometimes it's a need you have prayed for; sometimes it's a need you didn't even know you had. But God knows things about your future that you cannot see. Trust him enough to spontaneously accept his sudden interventions. Spontaneity can be a blessing on the horizon if you allow the light of his presence to shine upon each moment.

- Suddenly God can come along beside you.

As they talked and discussed these things, Jesus himself suddenly came and began walking with them.

Luke 24:15

- Suddenly God can interrupt your day.

Suddenly the LORD called out, "Samuel!" "Yes?" Samuel replied. "What is it?"

1 Samuel 3:4

- Suddenly God can do a new thing in your life.

Forget the former things; do not dwell on the past. See, I am doing a new thing! Now it springs up; do you not perceive it?

Isaiah 43:18–19 NIV

- Suddenly God can tear down everything that hinders your relationship with him.

The light from the sun was gone. And suddenly, the curtain in the sanctuary of the Temple was torn down the middle.

Luke 23:45

- Suddenly God can fill your atmosphere with his presence.

Suddenly, there was a sound from heaven like the roaring of a mighty windstorm, and it filled the house where they were sitting.

Acts 2:2

- Suddenly God can reveal to you the magnitude of his power.

Now it happened, when the congregation had gathered against Moses and Aaron, that they turned toward the tabernacle of meeting; and suddenly the cloud covered it, and the glory of the LORD appeared.

Numbers 16:42

- Suddenly God can intervene within your situation.

Suddenly, the glory of the God of Israel appeared from the east. The sound of his coming was like the roar of rushing waters, and the whole landscape shone with his glory.

Ezekiel 43:2

- Suddenly assistance can come from an unexpected source.

Then as he lay and slept under a broom tree, suddenly an angel touched him, and said to him, "Arise and eat."

1 Kings 19:5 NKJV

- Suddenly God can speak peace into your storm.

When Jesus woke up, he rebuked the wind and said to the waves, "Silence! Be still!" Suddenly the wind stopped, and there was a great calm.

Mark 4:39

- Suddenly God can move you into a position to advance.

When the people heard the sound of the rams' horns, they shouted as loud as they could. Suddenly, the walls of Jericho collapsed, and the Israelites charged straight into the town and captured it.

Joshua 6:20

• Suddenly you can be free from the ties that bind you.

Suddenly, there was a massive earthquake, and the prison was shaken to its foundations. All the doors immediately flew open, and the chains of every prisoner fell off!

Acts 16:26

• God is the God of suddenly moments.

Go back to what you heard and believed at first; hold to it firmly. Repent and turn to me again. If you don't wake up, I will come to you suddenly, as unexpected as a thief.

Revelation 3:3

Detachment—*Cut the Ties (Snip, Snip)*

You are a fluid creation. Inside of you are cells, neurons, and hormones in constant movement. Your mind is continually sending, storing, and receiving information. Your body responds spontaneously to the directions sent down from your master control centers. Each system is receptive of input from the other and strengthened by the information gained. They have merged into one cohesive unit. They have developed a level of complete codependence. If one system fails it causes strain and dysfunction in the others, so we must take care to keep all flowing smoothly.

Like your mind and your body, your soul has a master control center. There is a heavenly flow of continuous information being sent down for your benefit. How much you partake of that flow depends upon your openness to receive. Place

151

yourself daily in a position to be receptive to divine interventions in your life. Be sensitive to the situations around you and look for the potential in each moment. Allow a spontaneous "Yes God" to arise each time he asks you to expand your expectations. Release your hold on your plans and accept the movement of God's timing. In some instances you may have to complete a time of preparation and waiting, but never forget the power of *suddenly*.

Emotions

13

Emotional Imbalance Is Only for Crazy Women

"I should have castrated him in his sleep when I had the chance."

April was rocking back and forth on the edge of her chair in a futile attempt to calm herself. Anger, disappointment, fear, anxiety, and depression were the results of Jeremy's infidelity. The reality of his affair was still fresh in her mind. Nothing had prepared her for the betrayal and pain she felt. His preference for another had awakened old feelings of insecurity and self-doubt. She spent many nights lying awake agonizing over what the future would hold as the single parent of a ten-year-old and a seven-year-old. Her life had entered a series of successive changes, each leaving little time for adjustment.

"Twelve years!" she exclaimed. "After twelve years he decides he doesn't love me anymore. Now what am I supposed to do?"

April was more than a patient, she was my friend. Knowing how much Jeremy's thoughtless actions had hurt her made it difficult for me to act unbiased. Emotional pain has a way of permeating a room, leaving behind just enough potency to infect the person with you if that person is not careful. April's anger and anxiety were quickly attempting to claim anyone close enough to listen to the account of her pain.

"I really think I may need to see a psychiatrist," she confessed. "I can't get the image of the two of them out of my mind. It's as if our marriage held no significance for him. He barely calls the kids or comes over to see them. I cannot believe how easily he moved on. Why can't I move on? Am I going crazy, Saundra?"

"Crazy? No, I don't think you're going crazy. You do have a lot of emotions you are trying to figure out."

"I just don't know how to get my life back together," April continued. "I feel so off balance, as if my world has been turned upside down. My heart actually aches! It's as if he tore out a part of me. I just don't know where to begin."

April and Jeremy's divorce had been finalized for six months. Jeremy was now living with his mistress, while April was left to piece together her life and the lives of her children. The betrayal had evoked a nauseating wave of emotional pain over all those standing in its path. April needed a lifeline to help pull what remained of her household back onto solid emotional ground.

"April, you need to have an affair of your own." I smiled.

"What? I just went through a messy divorce. My kids are in turmoil about their father's behavior, and your suggestion is I jump in bed with another man!" April's raised eyebrows echoed the surprise in her voice.

"Now hear me out, April. I know it sounds a little crazy on my part, but you need a dose of love and affection. The best way to mend a broken heart is to refill it with love. Nothing I know feels as good as falling in love, so why not find someone who can replace what you've lost?"

April stared at me in disbelief, unsure if she could believe her ears. After contemplating my comments, she finally started laughing uncontrollably. "I don't know which of us needs that psychiatrist the most. Since you brought it up, I assume there must be someone specific you are trying to set me up with?"

"It depends on what you're looking for. What exactly do you want in a man?" I probed.

She thought for some time, tapping her finger on her lips as she cataloged wants from needs. Basing her choice for a life partner on good looks and a smooth line had ended in disaster. Now she truly thought about what qualities were important. "He should be nice, compassionate, good with kids, fun to be around, a good personality, responsible, and capable of being faithful."

It felt good to see some reflection of her former happiness as she imagined her ideal soul mate. I pulled a seat up close to April, excited for the chance to tell her about the great guy I had in mind.

"I actually do have someone I think is perfect for you," I admitted. "It's someone you actually have met in the past, but I don't think you saw him as lover material."

April searched my face for any hint about the mystery man. Her nervous fidgeting had now calmed as she reassigned her energies to this new mental task. Unable to guess his name, she finally asked, "Well, don't keep me in suspense. Who is he?"

"I certainly don't want to keep you in suspense. He's everything you mentioned and a whole lot more. He goes by a lot of names such as Adonai, Elohim, El-Shaddai, and Emmanuel, but I simply like to call him Jesus."

April's mouth hung open as all traces of her smile vanished. "You know I don't believe in any of that. What can Jesus do for me? He can't get my husband back. He can't pay my bills. He can't hold me at night when I'm lonely. He couldn't even keep my husband from cheating!"

"Did you ask him to?"

April and I sat only inches from each other, a closeness that signified the intimacy of our friendship, yet both of us shifted uncomfortably, uneasy with where this conversation was leading. April's hands opened and closed as she mulled over the question posed to her. We both knew the answer was no.

"You're right, April. He's not going to rain dollars down from heaven to pay your bills, and he may not bring Jeremy back. We will never know if he could have kept your husband from cheating, because he was never asked for help. But there is a lot he can do for you and a lot you need him to do. When you are alone at night, he is present. You can confide in him. You can trust him with your fears and insecurity about the future, and in exchange he is able to calm those feelings. You yourself even said you need a counselor, so why not start with him? If you can't see him as the lover of your soul, can you at least believe he wants to be your friend? You were ready to go out on a date with whatever nice guy I was ready to tell you about. What about Jesus? Can I set you up on a date with Jesus?"

My young atheist friend was at a loss for words. Long ago, I had stopped asking her to go to church with me because the rhetoric of religion had driven her away from church pews. What I needed her to see now was that Jesus was accessible to her right where she was, whether it was in her living room, in her kitchen, or in my office. She needed a *One Night with the King* experience to take her from the place of spiritual distance where she currently resided to a place of intimacy and relationship.

"Just say yes, April," I urged. "All I am asking is for you to give him a chance. What have you got to lose?"

There were no smiles, no hint of any change in April's disposition on the matter. She just continued to stare at me without a word, as if in some type of spiritual shock. We sat there side by side, neither of us saying a word. Finally April sat up straight, shaking her head. "Nothing. I have nothing to lose. The things I cared about have already been lost, so why not. Okay, what is it you want me to do? Go to church with you this Sunday to meet Jesus? What exactly do you have in mind?"

Every part of me wanted to shout for joy for this small opening. "No church involved. It's a date, just you and Jesus. Why don't you go home and freshen up and set a table for two. I'll drop by to pick up the kids at six for a slumber party at my place. Then the two of you can get reacquainted."

April laughed a harsh, mocking sound. "Whatever. I could use a night of peace and quiet. I'll see you at six."

⟨⊙⟩⟨⊙⟩

The kids were oblivious to the tense exchange at the door, too excited to care. They grabbed their overnight bags and rushed past me to the car.

"Well, where is he?" April waved her hand around in jest.

"He's waiting for you to invite him in. He's not going to attack you, April. He's not going to force himself on you. He is a gentleman. You must make the first move. If you want to begin healing that ache in your heart, then he is ready to listen."

I walked past her and quickly began setting the atmosphere for intimacy in her dining room. I dimmed the lights and lit the candles. An arrangement of fresh flowers was on the table. I divided takeout between two plates. My friend stared, amused at how far I had gone to prepare for her date. As she walked me to the door, she finally asked, "What am I supposed to do? Just eat? How does this work?"

"You talk to him the same way you would to me, but without any inhibitions. Say the things you have always wanted to say to him. Say them out loud. There is no one here but the two of you, no need for shame or fear. No need to pretend. Just be truthful. And just in case you don't know where to begin, open this to the places I have labeled."

April took my Bible in her hands. She flipped it open to the first red tab and read the highlighted passage. The tearful glaze in her eyes was my sign that he had entered the room. It was time for me to leave the two of them alone.

Lie #6: Emotional Imbalance Is Only for Crazy Women

Life can be unpredictable. From the mountaintop moments of joy to the depths of our soul-searching valleys, changes throw our emotions to and fro. Without an anchor to brace us against the jarring waves of emotions, it is easy to feel unstable, insane, and a little crazy at times.

The defining point between those with true mental illness and those experiencing temporary mental distress is the degree of change from baseline to precipice. True insanity takes you to the edge of reality and plummets you into a state of continual false perception. However, many women have situational depression and anxiety based on life events. Situational emotions are amenable to change through psychological and spiritual counseling. This type of temporary mental lapse does not mean you are crazy but rather that you are vulnerable to an emotional attack.

An emotional attack is similar to a heart attack. Many events have to become aligned prior to an actual heart attack. Years before a cardiac event, the blood vessel has to have an area of injury. It becomes inflamed and irritated after the injury. The area tries to heal the best way it can, so fatty tissue attaches to patch up the injured site. This extra padding inside the vessel causes the diameter of the vessel to constrict, which leads to less blood flow and less of the life-giving energy needed to keep it alive. Similarly, when you have an emotional attack there has to be an initial area of injury—a divorce, a job loss, or a death. The pain of the event causes you to become anxious and irritated. You try to hold it all together the best way that you can, often compensating with things that only clog and constrict your ability to tap into God's love. Over time the deficit reaches a critical limit where permanent injury will ensue without intervention.

This lie suggests that everyone is able to keep his or her emotions in check at all times. This could not be further from the truth. My experience has been that everyone has good and bad days, highs and lows, joy and sorrow. No one is exempt from the changes of life. Feeling depressed at times does not mean you have the clinical form of depression. Being anxious about something does not suggest you need immediate psychiatric admission. The clinical forms of depression and anxiety occur when these feelings become debilitating. If these emotions persist over a few consecutive weeks, they intrude upon your ability to live life and require medical treatment. However, these emotions also occur in mentally healthy people who have unfortunately experienced a transient emotional attack.

How do you heal an emotional attack? You must restore the flow of life-giving energy, just like when treating a heart attack. When someone presents to the ER with a heart attack, every effort is made to open the closed artery as quickly as possible. Doctors give blood thinners, administer oxygen, and anesthetize the pain until they can view the patient's arteries by catheterization. Halting an emotional attack also requires the restoration of blood flow. There is life-sustaining power to live freely by the blood of Christ. Our emotions require resuscitation to recover from attacks and to burst forth alive and new.

Illumination—*Peek Inside Yourself*

Medication can treat an emotional attack temporarily, but for sustained results the flow of grace, mercy, love, peace, and joy must return to your vital organs. Recognizing the onslaught of an emotional attack can help prevent permanent damage.

Do any of the following statements describe you?

- I tend to focus on the negative more than the positive.
- I feel sad more than 50 percent of the time.
- I sometimes feel guilty and worthless.
- Sometimes I find myself just going through the motions instead of fully enjoying things.
- If I have a bad day I feel tired and fatigued.
- I find it hard to cope with things that used to be manageable.
- I often wake up at night with bad dreams.
- Since my (divorce, loss job, etc.), I no longer feel confident in that area of my life.
- I worry about what the future holds for me.
- I am restless and easily irritated by others.
- I have trouble falling asleep because I can't get my mind to quiet down.

- I'm often fidgety, wring my hands, or need to shift how I am sitting.
- I have lost interest in activities I once enjoyed.

None of these statements alone are cause for immediate concern, but having five or more indicates a potential problem. The initial injury has occurred. The resulting emotional pain has caused an inflammatory response in your spirit, and the arteries of your soul are beginning to harden. Now is the time to take action to prevent an emotional attack before it is too late.

Activation—*Change Is Hard Work and It May Involve Sweat*

What differentiates those who go through the devastations of life mentally intact from those who suffer nervous breakdowns? What mental reserves do these overcomers have that help them surf the tides of their emotions? How do they keep it all together when life throws a stone at their glass house? They don't. They can no more keep it all together than you or I. But rather than cling to the glass that's shattering around them, they anchor themselves into a foundation. They stabilize their emotions by attaching the power of their emotions to a higher power.

As easy as this may sound, it is actually very difficult. It requires a spiritual relationship that views God not as a fatherly disciplinarian but as Jesus, an approachable friend and confidant. Growing up I had a very easy time discussing my feelings with my friends but would never have imagined telling my father the ups and downs of female adolescence. Often we shy away from opening up to God to discuss our feelings. When is the last time you said, "God, I'm mad at you! How could you let this happen?" or "God, what are you doing?" We can easily express these types of statements between close friends, and it helps to keep the relationship pure. When pretense and ritual replace communication, the relationship suffers and weakens.

Weak relationships are the result of a weak foundation. When trouble shakes the foundation of your soul, you learn very quickly whether your foundation is strong enough to maintain your equilibrium. Even good foundations can crack, but a crack will not cause you to crumble to the ground. Cracks can be repaired and foundations can be refortified. Spend time building up your relationship with the One who is able to support you through the good and the bad.

Transition—*Stretched to the Max but Rebounding with Grace*

How far have you allowed your relationship with God to go? Is it possible that instead of a relationship you merely have an association? I have associations with many people I work with. I see them at work, but we don't make an effort to see each other outside of office hours. I don't call to speak with them on the phone, and if I don't see or hear from them for a week, it doesn't cause me any concern. On the other hand, I am in an intimate relationship with my husband. I think about him when we are not together. We send messages to each other throughout our work days. I can tell him my hopes and dreams without shame, and I can be vulnerable without the fear of being abused. I am in love with him. No matter how much I love my husband, though, he cannot stabilize my emotions. For this to occur, I must have a love relationship with Jesus.

How strong is your foundational relationship? What is your level of intimacy with Jesus? When was the last time

163

you spent the day sending up small prayers of love and adoration just because the thought of him brought a smile to your face? Does your heart long for him when an extended period of time has passed without communion? Has it been a long time since you have told him your hopes and dreams? Do you trust him with your fears and anxieties? When is the last time you had a date with Jesus? Spend some time reading his love letters to you. He is ready to meet with you, but you must make the first move. There is no emotion capable of overcoming his love.

> The best and most beautiful things in the world cannot be seen or even touched. They must be felt with the heart.
>
> Helen Keller

14

My Transparency Opens the Door for Soul Connections

If you knew me—really knew me—what is the possibility that we could be friends? Can I trust you with my feelings and emotions? What would you think about my fears and insecurities? Would they become ammunition for your gossip and fuel for your ridicule? Do we have anything in common? Do you enjoy travel or music or movies? Could we converse over a latte about our dreams and ambitions? Would you think less of me if you knew about my past failures and weaknesses? How much can I share with you? How much would you share with me? Do I dare let you peek inside at the real me? Should I remove the mask of pretense that you have grown so fond of? What would happen if I allowed myself to be vulnerable? This could be risky, but I think it's worth the investment.

If you were honest with yourself, how many people would you say you are totally transparent with? I would bet the number is very low; for some, the number may be zero. Being transparent can be a frightening proposal. Transparency is being open and forthcoming about every aspect of your life—your emotions, fears, successes, failures, and everything in between laid out for inspection. No pretense, no lies, no coatings to make it more palatable; transparency means that what you see is what you get. It is your authentic self without any social makeup applied to make you look better. It is who you are when you are alone with yourself.

Transparency requires us to tear down the walls of protection that we have erected to protect ourselves from emotional pain and embarrassment. It expands the boundaries we set within our relationships. Transparency moves us from a superficial level of communication to the point of true connection. "Therefore each of you must put off falsehood and speak truthfully to his neighbor, for we are all members of one body" (Eph. 4:25 NIV). Once truth pierces the outer shells of our personalities, it becomes easier to see the similarities within our life experiences. These types of soul connections lead to mutually gratifying relationships. Each person feels safe being open and honest. Each feels that her position within the relationship is secure, regardless of the information shared. There is no fear of rejection, because the shared love and admiration cast out all thoughts of fear. The transparent emotional tape that holds the two people together creates a connection so strong that no matter how disturbing the subject matter, they are committed to sticking it out together. Transparency builds relationships that have the ability to withstand both the good and the bad.

It would not be advisable to be transparent with everyone you meet. Have you ever had a complete stranger start telling you intimate details about their marriage or health? It creates a level of discomfort because we are not accustomed to people being transparent. It makes you want to draw back and put up a sign that says "too much information." You should not practice transparency with every person you meet in the grocery store checkout or at the gas station, but it is important to seek opportunities to connect with those who have things in common with you. People you interact with daily are often an excellent resource when practicing transparency. A commonality allows you opportunities to share, and transparency allows a deeper knowledge of each other. These types of relationships have the potential to develop into lasting friendships.

Risky Business

Transparency is risky business. Sharing personal information puts you in a vulnerable position. It communicates that you trust this individual not to abuse the access you have allowed. If access to our fears, insecurities, and secret thoughts got into the wrong hands it could lead to a deep wounding through betrayal and humiliation. For this reason, many people have decided there is never a time to be transparent—not with spouses, not with children, not with friends, and not with God. Such people carry on every conversation from a distance, only allowing others to get close enough to hear what they are saying but not close enough to see who they are. This distance is functional and can maintain relationships for months and years. However, problems will begin to arise when there is a lack of continual exchange.

Active communication requires interesting dialogue, and hearing only about someone's successes has a tendency to close the door on dialogue so that it becomes a monologue. When we do not share more about ourselves with others, it causes them to create their own story about who we are, which is often an idealistic, flawed story. Opening up those areas of life that are still a work in progress can lead to an exchange of thoughts and ideas and the opportunity to learn from each other's mistakes as well as successes.

Imagine each acquaintance you meet as a book on a shelf. At first glance you may look at the superficial elements: the cover design, the size of the book, whether it's a hardcover or paperback. Once you find a book that appears pleasing, you will likely flip it over to read the back cover. The first time you meet someone at your company picnic or on a first date are "back cover" encounters. You don't really know what you are going to get, but you get a good glance at what the acquaintance wants you to think about him or her. This back cover phase of relationships hides most of our short-comings from view. Such relationships share little deep and meaningful information, but you learn a lot of nice stuff. If you like what you find on the cover, you will take the time to go deeper into the content.

I call the next level of discovery the plot phase. In this phase of a relationship, we gain additional information about each other as we lay the foundations of who we are, taking great care not to disclose too much negative information. We may share small failures in order to gauge the reaction and the level of acceptance established thus far in the relationship. This is where many relationships come to a halt. If the reaction is different than your expectation, it's unlikely that you will disclose more intimate details. But if the reaction is favorable or, better yet, reciprocal, a connection begins to develop, and we move toward the unveiling.

The unveiling phase is like that part in a great mystery novel where you can't put the book down. You need to sleep, but even sleep doesn't sound as good as finding out more clues about the mystery. In this part of building relationships, we want to find ways to get back into the presence of the one being unveiled. Her mysteries cause a sense of adventure that draws us into her. We want to know the deep secrets hidden within the pages of her life. We consume this information as one wanting to understand and not as one wanting to judge. We are excited at the opportunity to put the puzzle pieces together that will reveal the real character of the one being unveiled. It is at this phase that lifelong connections are created. Just like with a good book, we want to share this amazing find with others because we have taken something away from our time with that person.

If most of our relationships are stopping at the back cover phase or the plot phase, how do we get to the point of building these long-lasting relationships? At some point in the telling of your story, you have to show up and become an active participant. Until there is some level of unveiling, friendships stay superficial and shallow. We love having someone to turn to when life gets hard, someone who will listen to our cares without acting superior; someone who can console us when things don't turn out as we had hoped; someone with whom we can share our trials when in need of prayer. To get that type of relationship, we have to be willing to pull back the layers we have wrapped ourselves in.

Self-Disclosure

Self-disclosure is your willingness to share more about yourself with others. It requires self-acceptance and self-confidence. It requires letting go of the fear of rejection. It should be a reciprocal process where vulnerability is met by equal sharing of experiences. If your defense mechanisms go up to protect yourself against possible embarrassment, that shows a lack of trust within the relationship. That lack of trust can be directly related to the person you are interacting with, but often it relates to past experiences with others.

Past emotional wounding is the main roadblock to self-disclosure. Pain can erect a relationship-blocking wall where nothing comes in and nothing goes out. It causes us to halt in our tracks when we are about to share sensitive information but want to determine whether it's safe to proceed. Depending on the depth of the emotional breach, getting beyond this roadblock can be difficult. Some of the most interesting women I've ever met have gone through some of the most painful experiences you could imagine. Yet through their pain they have come to a point of acceptance and belief that their pain, their trials, their hardships are not judgments on their lives but rather events that they can learn from and help others learn from.

Self-disclosure is your opportunity to open the pages of your personal life story. It's always easier to share the parts of your life that are wonderful and perfect, but what about those things behind the veil? What about the part of your story that has a sense of mystery and suspense? Pull to the surface those experiences that are unthinkable and horrific. Recall those things you wish had never occurred and could be erased forever from your record. Bring forth those times when life took a turn you did not expect. Now, rather than finding more walls to use as barricades for these issues, uncover a way to redeem the past. Your past disappointments are not a judgment on your life. Your past failures are not an indication of your future experiences. Your past wounds do not have to be a continued source of pain.

Self-disclosure can take place in various ways, and it has the power to liberate the places where you hurt the worst. Join a group of others who feel pain in those same areas of life and share your experience with them. Call someone who is going through a similar situation and offer an ear. When you communicate your personal account of how something has affected you, you provide the other person freedom to share her story. Before you know what has happened, connections are forming and relationships are created that go beyond the back cover level, past the plot phase, and into the unveiling of the wisdom you contain.

Expulsion—*Dynamic Interference Required*

No one can know a person's thoughts except that person's own spirit, and no one can know God's thoughts except God's own Spirit. And we have received God's Spirit (not the world's spirit), so we can know the wonderful things God has freely given us.

1 Corinthians 2:11–12

Transparency builds relationship, and God desires to build his relationship with you. He desires to reveal himself to you. His Spirit knows the mysteries that he has in his heart, and that Spirit resides in you in order to disclose those mysteries to you.

For many years I thought the disappointing things that happened in my life were in some way a punishment from God. Our relationship was distant at best, and in all honesty, completely nonexistent at one point. Past mistakes and hurts seemed like an insurmountable wall. I could not imagine being transparent with anyone and certainly not with God. Every relationship in my life was affected by the distance between my words and my heart. I had a fear of being transparent. Fear is an unusual emotion. It is only as powerful as the fuel you feed it. If you feed it negative, self-defeating thoughts, it will grow. But if you surround it with affirmation, self-acceptance, and the truth of God's Word, it loses its hold on your life.

There are times in our lives when we must come face-to-face with God, times when our relationship with him will not grow until we are able to come to him with our feelings. During these times we learn the power of God's love for us. Disappointments and losses in our lives do not change the character of God. God is good. God is merciful. God is love. If you find it hard to be transparent with others, first learn how to be transparent with him. He knows about every aspect of your life and still wants to be the lover of your soul.

- I am being pursued.

Yes, I have loved you with an everlasting love; Therefore with lovingkindness I have drawn you.

Jeremiah 31:3 NKJV

- God is calling me to a deeper relationship.

Are you tired? Worn out? Burned out on religion? Come to me. Get away with me and you'll recover your life. I'll show you how to take a real rest. Walk with me and work with me—watch how I do it. Learn the unforced rhythms of grace. I won't lay anything heavy or ill-fitting on you. Keep company with me and you'll learn to live freely and lightly.

Matthew 11:28–30 Message

- My life is transparent before God.

O LORD, you have examined my heart and know everything about me. You know when I sit down or stand up. You know my thoughts even when I'm far away. You see me when I travel and when I rest at home. You know everything I do. You know what I am going to say even before I say it, LORD.

Psalm 139:1–4

• Fear is not from God.

For God has not given us a spirit of fear and timidity, but of power, love, and self-discipline.

2 Timothy 1:7

• Fear is my call to seek intimacy.

Such love has no fear, because perfect love expels all fear. If we are afraid, it is for fear of punishment, and this shows that we have not fully experienced his perfect love.

1 John 4:18

• God is love.

We know how much God loves us, and we have put our trust in his love. God is love, and all who live in love live in God, and God lives in them.

1 John 4:16

• I can freely approach God.

In him and through faith in him we may approach God with freedom and confidence.

Ephesians 3:12 NIV

• God is not angry with me.

But you, O Lord, are a God of compassion and mercy, slow to get angry and filled with unfailing love and faithfulness.

Psalm 86:15

• My past is not a barrier between us.

How great is God's love for all who worship him? Greater than the distance between heaven and earth! How far has the LORD taken our sins from us? Farther than the distance from east to west!

Psalm 103:11–12 CEV

• God is waiting on me.

Listen! I am standing and knocking at your door. If you hear my voice and open the door, I will come in and we will eat together.

Revelation 3:20 CEV

• God loves me unconditionally.

Can anything ever separate us from Christ's love? Does it mean he no longer loves us if we have trouble or calamity, or are persecuted, or hungry, or destitute, or in danger, or threatened with death? . . . I am convinced that nothing can ever separate us from God's love. Neither death nor life, neither angels nor demons, neither our fears for today nor our worries about tomorrow—not even the powers of hell can separate us from God's love. No power in the sky above or in the earth below—indeed, nothing in all creation will ever be able to separate us from the love of God that is revealed in Christ Jesus our Lord.

Romans 8:35, 38–39

• I can seek God in my place of weakness.

174

Have mercy on me, O God, because of your unfailing love. Because of your great compassion, blot out the stain of my sins. Wash me clean from my guilt. Purify me from my sin.

Psalm 51:1–2

- God will never abandon me.

I will never leave you nor forsake you.

Hebrews 13:5 NKJV

- I am not alone in my trials.

Do not be afraid, for I have ransomed you. I have called you by name; you are mine. When you go through deep waters, I will be with you. When you go through rivers of difficulty, you will not drown. When you walk through the fire of oppression, you will not be burned up; the flames will not consume you. For I am the LORD, your God.

Isaiah 43:1–3

- God is continually thinking about me.

How precious are your thoughts about me, O God. They cannot be numbered! I can't even count them; they outnumber the grains of sand!

Psalm 139:17–18

- God is aware of every tear I've cried.

You have kept record of my days of wandering. You have stored my tears in your bottle and counted each of them.

Psalm 56:8 CEV

- God's love can overcome every difficulty.

Love is invincible facing danger and death. Passion laughs at the terrors of hell. The fire of love stops at nothing—it sweeps everything before it. Flood waters can't drown love, torrents of rain can't put it out.

Song of Solomon 8:7 Message

- God has chosen me.

You did not choose Me, but I chose you and appointed you that you should go and bear fruit, and that your fruit should remain, that whatever you ask the Father in My name He may give you.

John 15:16 NKJV

- I bring great joy to God.

For the LORD your God is living among you. He is a mighty savior. He will take delight in you with gladness. With his love, he will calm all your fears. He will rejoice over you with joyful songs.

Zephaniah 3:17

- There is an invitation before me.

The LORD said: It isn't too late. You can still return to me with all your heart.

Joel 2:12 CEV

- I choose to accept God's love.

It was but a little that I passed from them, when I found him whom my soul loveth: I held him, and would not let him go.

Song of Solomon 3:4 ASV

- God's love completes me.

May you experience the love of Christ, though it is too great to understand fully. Then you will be made complete with all the fullness of life and power that comes from God.

Ephesians 3:19

- Our relationship will deepen in the secret place of his presence.

He who dwells in the secret place of the Most High shall abide under the shadow of the Almighty. I will say of the LORD, "He is my refuge and my fortress; My God, in Him I will trust."

Psalm 91:1–2 NKJV

- God is passionately pursuing me.

Surely your goodness and unfailing love will pursue me all the days of my life.

Psalm 23:6

- Now I will passionately pursue him.

I am my beloved's and his desire is toward me. Come, my beloved, let us go forth into the field.

Song of Solomon 7:10–11 ASV

Detachment—*Cut the Ties (Snip, Snip)*

You are known by God. But God does not just want to know you; he desires a transparent relationship with you. He seeks a level of intimacy with you that will lead to open conversations about your joy and your pain. He wants you to invite him into your times of sorrow. He yearns for entry into the areas of your life that need to be revived with his presence. He wants to celebrate with you during times of triumph.

177

His love for you is indescribable. It goes beyond all you can imagine. There is nothing that can stand between you and God's love. Not even the life of his only son, Jesus. Every barrier that has formed, every sin you have committed, every mistake you have made, every wall you have erected can become obsolete under the liberating flow of God's grace and love. Allow God an unobstructed view into your feelings. Become transparent with the One who is able to breathe life into your relationships. One moment of transparency can heal a lifetime of pain.

Limits

15

Everything Comes with Conditions

"Cameron?" Shannon called into the waiting room.

Her voice pierced through Cameron's mental fog as she beckoned her to come back to the exam room. Five months later and twenty pounds lighter, Cameron was successfully on her way to overcoming the many areas of her life that had prevented her from living free. She had recommitted her life to Christ and was actively seeking a deeper relationship with God. No longer did she fear what the future held but embraced the opportunity to enjoy the spontaneous aspects of life. She had found that eating more natural foods allowed her to lose weight without feeling deprived and that playing chase with the kids was great exercise. Her priorities not only included taking care of those she loved but also adequate time for self-care. Despite all of her progress though, Cameron still battled with one issue that was going to be a difficult one for her to conquer.

The warm smile that spread across her face as I entered the room was a telling sign of the bond we had made over the past months. The tense debate of our initial encounter was a thing of the past. An open and blunt exchange was the norm between us now and both expected nothing less. As was our routine, I had given Cameron a pre-appointment assignment at her last visit. Her assignment was to write down the things she would ask from God if she could have anything. There were no limitations. They could be material, emotional, relational, physical, past, present, or future. What would she want from God if she could pick her specific blessings?

"Cameron, I feel like this is graduation day for you!" I smiled as I sat in the chair across from her. "You are a different person from the woman that walked in here months ago."

Cameron was lighter in every aspect of her life. Joy had elevated her emotions. Peace had lifted her psychological heaviness. Spiritual and physical weight had dropped from her body and soul. "I am a different person," she concluded.

In her hands she held her pink and blue striped journal. On the cover she had taped a picture of her family and on the back she had taped her favorite Scripture passage. This journal held every lesson we had completed together. It contained her hopes, her fears, her disappointments, and her successes. Today it contained her spiritual wish list: everything she wanted to see God do in her life and in the life of her family.

"Well, let me see your list. What is it that you want from God?"

She flipped open her journal to the dated entry and handed it to me. One glance at the list confirmed my suspicions. I didn't read one word on the page nor did I flip to the next page. It was unnecessary. I had given Cameron an opportunity to ask God for whatever she desired. Some would call it a prayer list, others a life's desires list, but regardless of what you call the list, it was her chance to spell out what she would like to receive from God in her lifetime. I closed the book and handed it back to Cameron.

Cameron looked on in anticipation, awaiting my response to her list. When none was offered she asked, "What did you think about my list? I really thought about it a long time and tried to pick those things that were really important to me."

I had known today would be difficult, but I had no idea how difficult it was going to be. I was not prepared for what I found in Cameron's journal. In so many ways, Cameron reflected where I had been many years ago. Looking at her list was like looking down the corridor of my own past mental bondage.

"You are worth more than that," I stated simply.

Cameron stared at me, dumbfounded. The hurt in her eyes showed that whatever was on her list was very important to her, but regardless of what she had written down I could not get beyond the reality of it. She had limited herself to three desires. Three. Her life's desires list did not fill even one page of her journal. Nowhere in my instructions had I given her any limitations on the number of items she could include. At no time did I limit the type of concerns she could address. The assignment was left open for interpretation to see how bold Cameron would be in her requests, to see how much she could stretch her mind to encompass the unlimited potential she has available to her.

"Why did you stop at three? Are there really only three things you desire from God?" I implored, unable to believe it.

"Of course there are other things that are important to me . . . ," she began.

"Why did you stop at three?" I interrupted.

"I just picked the main things I wanted to see done."

"Why did you stop at three!" I almost shouted, overwhelmed by the mixture of emotions going through me. Anger began to rise as I mentally recounted all that this particular mental tie had cost me in my own life.

Cameron stopped talking long enough to actually think about the question. She stared at me with a questioning look, unsure of where the conversation was going. She opened the journal to her list and laid it on the table between us. Her hand spread over the words as if they in some way held the answer to my question.

"I did write another list," she admitted. "When you told me about this assignment, I started making a mental list and even jotted things down in the parking lot before leaving that day. I wrote and wrote desire after desire. The list was so long that I stopped numbering them. I was up to over fifty." She stopped and looked up at the ceiling. There was a long pause as she debated how to continue.

"Where is that list?" I questioned.

Cameron's gaze caught mine as she answered, "I threw it in the trash and started over."

Neither of us spoke for a moment as the irony of the action hit home.

"Cameron, the only limitations on your life are the ones you place on it. I asked you to write out your heart's desires. Those things that you would like to see God do in your life. Whether you were twenty or eighty years old, I would expect that list to be lengthy. God wants to lavish you with his goodness and every type of blessing you could imagine. If you think God would never do something great in your life, he probably will not. But if you could only dare to believe that God loves you enough to do the impossible in your life, your original list could become your testimony."

"God has never done all that before, so why should I set myself up for disappointment?" she admitted.

The words that Cameron had tried so hard to camouflage had slipped out in a moment of revealing truth. She stared down at the three phrases with which she had summarized her life's desires. The only sound in the room was the rhythmic clicking of her pen. The mental scars, fears, anxieties, and disappointments stemming from the pain of her past were still fresh. Despite her recent breakthroughs, she still did not feel God was trustworthy. God had not prevented Cameron's prior pain, and that breach of trust had not yet mended. She was so close to being free, yet remained grounded due to incremental feelings of mistrust.

"It's difficult when God allows things into our lives that we don't understand. It sometimes seems easier never to dream than to open yourself up to being let down. That's why it's important that your list be limitless and without restrictions. If your expectations are so narrow that there is only one way of completion, then you set yourself up for disappointment. When you've taken the restraints off of your expectations, you allow God the ability to create blessings out of your past disappointments. You give him the creative license to mold your broken pieces back into something wonderful. Do you believe that his plans for your future are good?"

"I do believe those things, but I looked at that original list and it just seemed ridiculous to think God would do all of those things in *my* life," she replied.

"Cameron, you are valuable to God and he wants you to trust him enough to ask. You will never receive some of the things you desire if you don't ask. Asking shows that you believe that he is capable of delivering what you have asked for. Receiving requires a willingness on your part to be vulnerable. You have to be willing to trust that the One giving the gifts knows you well enough to pick those things from your list that will give you the greatest joy."

"What if I don't get the things on my list?" she questioned. "You will continue to enjoy the new freedom you've found over the past five months. You don't have those things now and you are happier than I've ever seen you, so no harm done. But a better question is, what if you do get them? Think how seeing just one of your desires realized would affect you. Can you imagine the impact on not just your life but on that of your family? Can you imagine how it will affect your trust in God? What if you receive four or ten of your desires? There are so many blessings waiting on you to become free enough in your spirit to receive them. If you don't think God is able to do the things on your list, then don't bother writing them down. But if you believe it is possible, then you have prepared yourself to receive them."

"I think I need to redo my list." Cameron smiled. "There's a lot I want to see happen in my lifetime."

"Then this time write your list without limitation, without fear of conditions, without narrow expectations," I encouraged. "Open the door wide for every imaginable blessing to flood your life and even for some blessings your mind cannot comprehend. You are free to ask and free to receive God's best for your life."

Lie #7: Everything Comes with Conditions

Many areas of life have conditional clauses, a system of checks and balances to prevent an imbalance of power. The marriage relationship has parameters in which we must maintain a balanced account of giving and receiving of our time, love, and attention. We can only sustain our relationships with friends if there is an equal exchange of emotional resources. If one friend is always on the giving end and the other is always on the receiving end, eventually the friendship will suffer. Human relationships function best with conditional clauses, but to appreciate the relationship we have with God all such clauses must be null and void.

When you attempt to apply the same conditional clauses practiced in our human relationships with God, you set yourself up to feel unworthy of his blessings. How can you possibly keep up your end of a relational checks and balances system with the God of the universe? How long do you have to pray to earn that new job? How many hours of Scripture must you read to be healed? How loud do you have to sing to be released from anxiety? How many hours of charity work must you complete to deliver your child from addictions? What conference do you have to attend to get your breakthrough? How much money do you have to place in the offering to save your marriage?

Conventional conditions are not attached to the blessings God wants to bring into your life. The only requirement on your part is availability. Once he has extended his grace, you must be available to receive the blessing. Availability shows that you are easily accessible. It implies that there is receptiveness to his presence in your life. Trying to deliver a gift to someone encased in a wall of hurt and pain is a difficult task. However, God can easily lay a trail of gifts upon a path open for divine travel. Make yourself available to receive by being sensitive to God's interventions in your day-to-day activities. Being close to the Giver of all blessings puts you in the best possible position to see your prayers answered.

Illumination—*Peek Inside Yourself*

It's often said that it is better to give than to receive. This mentality has caused many to see receiving as an inferior activity. Have you ever tried to buy lunch for a friend and have her get offended, as if you were implying she could not afford the meal when in actuality you only wanted to bless her? Or have someone refuse a monetary gift when you both know the person would benefit from the extra funds? For some, receiving has become taboo except for the obligatory gifts at Christmas and birthdays. You greatly reduce your capacity to receive when you limit it to specific events and seasons.

Do any of the following statements describe you?

- I have trouble accepting compliments.
- I don't like getting gifts I did not expect.
- I am constantly giving to others but feel uncomfortable when others give to me.
- I often put others before myself.
- I feel more comfortable in the role of helper rather than being helped.
- I would rather blend in with the crowd than be singled out for recognition.
- I can easily give away things.
- I often feel that I have to work on myself to be good enough for more blessings in my life.
- I avoid situations where I would require receiving help from others.
- I have difficulty trusting others.
- I find it hard to say no to requests but would never request something from someone else.
- I believe it is better to give than to receive.
- When I spend more time in my Bible, I believe God is more likely to answer my prayers.

These statements show a pattern of imbalance in your ability to receive. Most of us have not learned how to receive gifts graciously. Receiving puts you in a vulnerable position. You are not in control of the specifics of the gift and you cannot dictate the timing of the gift. As the receiver, you are in a place of eager expectation depending on the giver's generosity. It is a place of trust and confirmation in your own self-worth. You are a valuable vessel to God and he wants to pour blessings into your life. Are you ready to receive them?

Activation—*Change Is Hard Work and It May Involve Sweat*

The common barriers to receiving include feelings of indebtedness, unworthiness, pride, and insecurity. These feelings cause an inability to accept gifts due to a belief that there are conditions attached. If you battle with feelings of indebtedness, you may feel that by receiving you will in some way owe something to the giver. For those with pride issues, the condition to receiving is neediness. If insecurity and unworthiness are the emotions blocking your ability to receive, you have adopted the mind-set that gifts must be earned.

It is easy to refuse a gift if you feel you have to work harder and become indebted and impoverished to get it. Fortunately, the gifts God wants to bring into your life come without baggage. They are free of conditions and await the opportune moment to surprise you. They can come from someone close to you or from a complete stranger. They can be tangible or intangible. They can be similar to the blessing your neighbor got or completely unique. The possible manifestations of your blessings are endless.

Gifts come in many forms, and it's necessary to learn how to accept them in their various presentations. Most of us have years of seasonal holiday giving to learn how to receive material gifts. The easiest gifts to receive are often those that we can wrap in a box. Many have a much harder time receiving verbal, physical, and spiritual gifts, yet these are the gifts with the greatest value. Verbal gifts of appreciation, affirmation, gratitude, and love are necessary to help remind us of our self-worth. Physical gifts of health, well-being, and wholeness are blessings from God that are priceless. The spiritual gifts of joy, peace, and hope can be some of the most difficult gifts to receive, but once obtained they have the potential to forever change your life.

Are you available to receive? What will you say the next time someone gives you an unexpected compliment? Can you accept words of affirmation and love graciously? How will you respond when a gift is extended to you just because someone wants to bless you? How will you answer when someone extends unrequested help? Are you ready to receive the answer to your prayers?

Transition—*Stretched to the Max but Rebounding with Grace*

Our capacity to give often characterizes our generosity; however, our capacity to receive can limit our ability to reciprocate. Giving is the window through which many blessings enter, but only if you do not slam the portal shut. There is an internal flow of God's grace carried down by every blessing, every kind word, and every selfless act. You are the reservoir he has chosen to carry this flow of his presence into the lives of others. When you lose your ability to receive, you dam up your potential and deprive others of the opportunity to drink the living water he has placed within you.

What do you desire from God? What areas of your life would you like to see him change for the better? Do not allow past disappointments to restrain you from anticipating something great from God. Allow yourself to stretch beyond the limits of your past expectations to a place of unlimited possibilities. Pinpoint your prayer at an area you would like to see touched by his gifts, but do not pigeonhole God into a specific way of fulfilling your desires. There are no limits, no boundaries, and no restraints on God. The limitations exist only in your mind. You have the ability to break free from every mind-set that is attempting to bind you. Experience the freedom of exploring uncharted territory with God. Experience the unlimited potential of God.

16

My Only Limitations Are the Ties I Allow to Bind Me

Life is an open invitation from God to experience the fullness of his power on earth. Each life is an opportunity to exhibit the unlimited ability of God to do what seems impossible. The vastness of God's authority within your life reaches to every area. There is not one aspect of your life, your career, your emotions, or your relationships that is unreachable. There are no limits to what he is able to do. The only limitations in our lives are the result of self-imposed boundaries. These boundaries limit our ability to see that God is able to overcome the circumstances of our lives. They are walls that we have erected and that restrict our ability to receive his unconditional love. These boundaries are the result of mental ties that constrict our freedom to live in the wide open space of God's grace. It is time to expand beyond every self-imposed limitation. It is time to cross over into the wide-open, spacious life God desires for us.

Mind Wide Open

Imagine a life with unlimited possibilities, with no limitations. A life free from the gravitational pull of your own insecurities, fears, and misconceptions. An open expanse of opportunities and experiences set before you, beckoning you to soar to new levels of fulfillment. An incredible overflowing display of endless possibilities extended upon a sea of grace. The only thing that can prevent you from walking into this new area is a lack of movement. The murky waters of uncertainty may not look strong enough to hold you up, but as you step out you will begin to feel the strength of God's promises keeping you afloat. Open your mind wide and allow God to enlarge your perception of what is before you.

Freedom begins in your mind. Your personal perception of the world, the events around you, and your status within these events influences the choices you make. Family beliefs, religion, education, media, and social relationships condition each of us. From an early age, these factors begin to form limitations in our minds. These boundaries diminish our ability to believe in things we have never experienced. They reduce our ability to believe anything is possible. Eventually life becomes so routine it no longer requires faith.

Faith is confidence in God's ability to do all he promises. It believes that there is a peace that surpasses all understanding available to us. It trusts in the goodness of God in every circumstance. It concludes that the end result of every equation is personal growth. It expects to find joy during times of worship. It anticipates strengthening during times of prayer. Faith is being sure of things you hope for and certain of things you do not yet see. It magnifies your vision so that you can see those things that are on the horizon. It allows room for God to elaborate upon the equation of your life.

"Without faith it is impossible to please God" (Heb. 11:6 NIV). His desire is to see you living daily in a realm of freedom and spontaneity. Leave behind both the fear of success and the fear of failure to move into all God has for you. Open up room for him to elaborate upon your life. Whether your life is going great or in need of a change, you should not leave him out of the equation. Allow your mind to be transformed and renewed. Extend your faith and see the impossible become a reality within your life. Open your mind wide to receive the mind and thoughts of God.

Eyes Wide Open

Vision can easily become distorted. Our eyes have a tendency to focus on the largest object in our visual field. As long as life is going well, it is easy to adapt to the ebbs and flows. Unfortunately, unexpected changes can come at any time, clouding our view. As these changes press upon us, it becomes difficult to focus on the big picture. Fear, anxiety, insecurity, and uncertainty can cloud our lens of perception. The pressures of career, family responsibilities, and financial obligations can increase to toxic levels that can blind us to the blessings right in front of us. The complications of bitterness, anger, and an unforgiving spirit can lead to bleeding within our relationships. With each insult, more vision is lost. Our visual field becomes compromised and reduced in size until eventually it is too small to see the greatness of God.

When you think about your life, your ambitions, and your goals, what do you see? Are your goals limited by what you think you are capable of? Have you placed limits on your ambitions due to perceived weaknesses? Have concerns about your prior education, your social standing, and your financial backing prevented you from seeking more? Are you paralyzed in your current state due to fear and anxiety?

People often say that seeing is believing. My experience has been that believing is seeing. You can choose to focus on what you see or on what you believe. Often what you see is only a fragment of the big picture. That particular piece of the puzzle you are currently seeing may be the darkest, most unattractive part of the picture. You can easily make a wrong decision if you base your perception of life on that part of the whole. But if your focus is on what you believe is true, even when confronted with an undesirable piece of your life's composition, you can maintain peace and contentment. When we refuse to see the truth, we begin to set up roadblocks that limit the flow of God in our lives. If your circumstances are not what you desire, your belief that all things work together for good can sustain you until you see goodness overtake the bad.

Open your eyes wide to the possibility that the life you've been living can be better. Expand the vision for your life to include abundant peace, abundant joy, and abundant grace. Receive a new perspective as the Word of God speaks new life into your spirit. Refresh your focus and see with improved clarity the view of your life from a higher vantage point. Allow the power within God's promises to remove every obstacle that has hindered your ability to see clearly. There is new vision available to those who believe they will see the grace and favor of God upon their lives. Open your eyes and see.

Arms Wide Open

When you believe God wants you to freely enjoy your life and you have renewed your vision, it is time to receive what you see. Receiving requires open hands. When your hands are open, it is very difficult to hold on to anything. Rather than things staying stagnant within your grasp they flow through you and around you. You become able to move unrestrained by things and circumstances. Possessions lose their power because you have the freedom to let go without feeling loss. Your trust in the One orchestrating the flow of events around you overcomes the fear of loss. You are able to build healthy relationships because you are open to embrace, and your movement liberates others to grow and develop without fear of abandonment. Blessings that seem so good you'll want to cling to them forever can be exchanged for blessings you cannot even imagine. How wide you can stretch dictates the magnitude of what you receive. Is the box in which you've placed God too small to receive the blessings you desire? Take a deep breath in, then exhale as you stretch your arms wide open to receive all God is releasing into your arms.

As a mother, my fondest moments with my sons were when they were toddlers. Picking them up at day care was the highlight of my day, not just because I would get to see them and hear about all they had done, but also because of how they made me feel. When I arrived at the first child's classroom door, one of his little classmates would usually announce my presence. From the corner I would hear a high-pitched squeal as my smiling toddler came running to me with arms stretched wide. The embrace was one of total abandon as his tiny body flung itself at me. There were no walls, no boundaries, and no limits. It did not matter who was watching or what they thought. The reunion was one of salutation, adoration, and praise. God loves to see us running to him with the same reckless abandon.

Stretch your arms wide as you take your hands off the steering wheel of your life. Allow God to have full control of your journey. Trust him to guide you to the best destinations.

Have confidence in his ability to take you through rough terrain. Believe that he is able to sustain you during times of uncertainty. Surrender fully to his loving embrace as he leaves the fragrance of his presence over your life. Press into the arms of the One who is able to surround your day with peace. Express your adoration to the One who is able to love you through your walls of insecurity. Allow praise to enlarge your territory as your love for him increases. Open arms are the pathway to an open heart.

Heart Wide Open

Inside of you throbs a pulsating wellspring of life. It's a well so rich, so deep, and so pure that its living water has the potential to quench every thirst. It's a powerful flow of healing and freedom ready to be released at a moment's notice from its home, your heart. Your heart is the deepest part of yourself. Behind the exterior walls, implanted deep inside of you, lies this divine network connecting your body to one common source. It joins your mind, your eyes, your arms, and your mouth. Whatever your heart contains will pump out into every part of your being.

Our hearts can become contaminated. They can become hardened by trials and difficult circumstances. They can be broken by grief and betrayal. They can become discouraged by delayed gratification. They can become deceived into believing lies over the truth. Therefore it is necessary to allow the life-giving blood of Jesus and the cleansing power of God's Word to decontaminate our hearts. Opening our hearts gives Jesus's blood access to those areas of our lives that have become defiled. He can then remove impurities from our systems. When we reconnect to the blood of Jesus, he can permanently release us and dispose of insecurity, fear, depression, and lost hope.

What you see flowing in your life is a direct result of what is flowing from your heart. Dysfunctional areas will lose their blood supply when you infuse the overcoming power of God. Allow a spring of expectation to begin to bubble up on the inside of you as you open your heart to God. Allow him to penetrate deep into the layers of your past contaminations. Treasure your time of purification and cleansing. Receive the inflow of his promises into the portals of your life. Accept his unconditional, unrestrained, untamed love for you with your heart wide open.

Expulsion—*Dynamic Interference Required*

Now open wide. God is ready to fill you with the Bread of Life. He has prepared meals and snacks of all sizes. Take as much as you need to feel satisfied. Each promise in his Word is like a fine meal or a decadent dessert that you need to savor. Allow them to roll around on your spiritual palate and fully experience the richness of each taste. Allow time for the contents of each meal to digest. Receive the nutrients released into your bloodstream. Allow the power of his blood to fill your heart. Each beat is releasing freedom as ties are being loosed and chains are being broken. Open your mouth wide and be fed from his hand of blessing.

- God wants to access every part of my life.

So here's what I want you to do, God helping you: Take your everyday, ordinary life—your sleeping, eating, going-to-work, and walking-around life—and place it before God as an offering. Embracing what God does for you is the best thing you can do for him.

Romans 12:1 Message

- Discontentment is an invitation to God's table.

Oh, Job, don't you see how God's wooing you from the jaws of danger? How he's drawing you into wide-open places— inviting you to feast at a table laden with blessings?

Job 36:16 Message

- God can enlarge my capacity to believe.

Don't copy the behavior and customs of this world, but let God transform you into a new person by changing the way you think. Then you will learn to know God's will for you, which is good and pleasing and perfect.

Romans 12:2

- The truth of God's Word calls me to action.

But be doers of the Word [obey the message], and not merely listeners to it, betraying yourselves [into deception by reasoning contrary to the Truth].

James 1:22 AMP

- I will open my heart to be purified.

Search me, O God, and know my heart; test me and know my anxious thoughts. Point out anything in me that offends you, and lead me along the path of everlasting life.

Psalm 139:23–24

- God's Word cleanses my mind and heart.

So that He might sanctify her, having cleansed her by the washing of water with the Word.

Ephesians 5:26 AMP

- I will open my ears to hear the voice of God.

Come to me with your ears wide open. Listen, and you will find life. I will make an everlasting covenant with you. I will give you all the unfailing love I promised to David.

Isaiah 55:3

- I will open my eyes wide to receive the light of God's glory.

No one lights a lamp, then hides it in a drawer. It's put on a lamp stand so those entering the room have light to see where they're going. Your eye is a lamp, lighting up your whole body. If you live wide-eyed in wonder and belief, your body fills up with light. If you live squinty-eyed in greed and distrust, your body is a dank cellar. Keep your eyes open, your lamp burning, so you don't get musty and murky. Keep your life as well-lighted as your best-lighted room.

Luke 11:33–36 Message

- What I see influences what I receive.

The LORD said to Abram after Lot had parted from him, "Lift up your eyes from where you are and look north and south, east and west. All the land that you see I will give to you and your offspring forever."

Genesis 13:14–15 NIV

- God wants me to ask for more.

And Jabez called on the God of Israel saying, "Oh, that You would bless me indeed, and enlarge my territory, that Your hand would be with me, and that You would keep me from evil, that I may not cause pain!" So God granted him what he requested.

1 Chronicles 4:10 NKJV

- God wants to satisfy my hunger.

Open your mouth wide, and I will fill it with good things.

Psalm 81:10

- I will open my mouth in anticipation of an outpouring.

They waited for me as for the rain, and they opened their mouth wide as for the spring rain.

Job 29:23 NKJV

- God is able to exceed all my expectations.

Now all glory to God, who is able, through his mighty power at work within us, to accomplish infinitely more than we might ask or think.

Ephesians 3:20

- God places me in a wide-open, spacious life.

But me he caught—reached all the way from sky to sea; he pulled me out of that ocean of hate, that enemy chaos, the void in which I was drowning. They hit me when I was down, but GOD stuck by me. He stood me up on a wide-open field; I stood there saved—surprised to be loved!

2 Samuel 22:17–20 Message

- Freedom is a testimony of God's grace.

Meditate on these things; give yourself entirely to them, that your progress may be evident to all.

1 Timothy 4:15 NKJV

- I will stand where I have always hoped to stand.

By entering through faith into what God has always wanted to do for us—set us right with him, make us fit for him—we have it all together with God because of our Master Jesus. And that's not all: We throw open our doors to God and discover at the same moment that he has already thrown open his door to us. We find ourselves standing where we always hoped we might stand—out in the wide open spaces of God's grace and glory, standing tall and shouting our praise.

Romans 5:1–2 Message

• My eyes will see the reality of my prayers.

Pray diligently. Stay alert, with your eyes wide open in gratitude.

Colossians 4:2 Message

• Nothing is impossible with God.

But Jesus looked at them and said to them, "With men this is impossible, but with God all things are possible."

Matthew 19:26 NKJV

Detachment—*Cut the Ties (Snip, Snip)*

I can't tell you how much I long for you to enter this wide-open, spacious life. We didn't fence you in. The smallness you feel comes from within you. Your lives aren't small, but you're living them in a small way. I'm speaking as plainly as I can and with great affection. Open up your lives. Live openly and expansively!

2 Corinthians 6:11–13 Message

The ties are loosed. The chains have been broken, the boundaries extended. There are no limits. Nothing is impossible. A wide-open, spacious life is before you.

PART 3

The Free Woman's Creed

17

The Diamond Society

At this point, you have become aware of some of the mental ties at work in your life. You've found the desire to be free and you've transitioned into a position for change. Now it's time to replace those old mental ties with a new perspective. It's time to adopt an enlightened belief system that embraces the freedom to enjoy individuality, spontaneity, and all of your unique attributes. God envisions a much bigger life for you than the life you have been living. Opportunities await you. You have talents yet to be discovered. The only things holding you back are your own misconceptions and false perceptions. It's time to be free from every tie that has bound you.

> Now the Lord is the Spirit, and where the Spirit of the Lord is, there is liberty (emancipation from bondage, freedom) [AMP]. So all of us who have had that veil removed can see and reflect the glory of the Lord. And the Lord—who is the

Spirit—makes us more and more like him as we are changed into his glorious image.

2 Corinthians 3:17–18

Life constantly offers opportunities for you to choose a mental perspective to embrace. Regardless of how intertwined some mental ties have become within your vision of life, the possibility of freedom remains a viable option. Let the floodgates of God's promises sweep through the mental debris of your past. Release your hold on those areas of your life that have become mundane and listless. Open your eyes, open your mind, open your heart, open your hands, and reach for that special place that God has reserved for you. Reach for that place where each day holds the potential to be breathtaking. Reach for that place where you are free to see even your past hurts, disappointments, and failures as a beautifully orchestrated crescendo in the song God is singing over you. The pivotal points of your life are where fracture lines occur and the chains of limitations begin to break.

God holds the keys to every type of bondage in your life. To be free you must allow his Spirit to have free reign. He has the power to heal as his Spirit comes into contact with old mental wounds. He has the ability to liberate you from condemnation when his Spirit confronts past failures. He has the capacity to strengthen you in the face of insecurity. Allow him to remove the veil and watch as he changes you into his image.

What lies have been holding you back from moving in the direction God has for you? What aspect of your life are you not enjoying to its fullest potential? What relationships have been missed due to fear of disclosure? What activities have you missed out on due to fears and phobias? What peace has been lost because you have become your own worst critic? Which mental tie has you bound?

The Seven Lies Women Tell Themselves

1. Perfection is the goal
2. I would be happy too if I had her life
3. If I do this, I can look like that
4. Life is an all-or-none activity
5. Being in control is better than spontaneity
6. Emotional imbalance is only for crazy women
7. Everything comes with conditions

For each lie there is a Bible-based promise to release you. As these new scriptural beliefs become embedded within your life, they will forcefully expel your old distorted perceptions and allow you to break free from past bondage. I call this renewed way of thinking the Free Woman's Creed. The seven proclamations in this creed have the power to release you into your destined freedom. You should incorporate this Free Woman's Creed into the way you view yourself and the way you relate to God and others. It will free you from your past limitations and open the door to peace, happiness, and contentment.

The Free Woman's Creed

1. I am perfectly imperfect
2. I am too unique for comparisons
3. My body, my temple, God's choice
4. My balanced life requires addition and subtraction
5. Spontaneity is God's opportunity to surprise me
6. My transparency opens the door for soul connections
7. My only limitations are the ties I allow to bind me

As you work through the components of the Free Woman's Creed, allow the purging of old thoughts from your mind. For some this process can become downright painful. Often the mental tie dominating your life is the one that will resist the most when you try to break free. You may have attempted to overcome this area in the past without success, but do not allow that to taint your current position. Old mental scars are linked to past failures, disappointments, and mistakes that become attached to other areas of your life. When these areas are pulled free from this tie, you can experience a temporary sense of vulnerability as you learn how to embrace your new freedom. Do not be intimidated. You will learn how to live outside the box of your past limitations.

One of the most liberating aspects of the Free Woman's Creed is that it does not require you to be perfect. No longer do you have to attempt to control every aspect of your life, but you can be confident that God is in control. You can rest in the knowledge of his love for you. You can be stable in your places of weakness as he strengthens you daily. You no longer need to seek the pretense of perfection but can bask in the peace of imperfection.

A Sisterhood of Overcomers

No one goes through life without ups and downs. Pressure and stress have a way of finding you even when you are sitting at the feet of Jesus. They are a part of every woman's experience; however, many women have become entombed by their intensity. Yet through all the fluctuations of life, there remains a group of women who are determined to take comfort in the promises of God. They have learned to embrace spontaneity and individuality. They know the value of transparency in their lives and its ability to help others.

They have made a choice to live their lives free from limiting thoughts and mind-sets. They are living examples of the Free Woman's Creed.

Many are superwomen managing home and career. Some of these women are battling cancer, some are single mothers, some are widows, some are mothers who have lost a child, and some are victims of past abuse. They range in age from early twenties to just over one hundred, and they include those receiving government assistance as well as those living in million-dollar homes. The one thing these women have in common is they all struggle with issues that threaten to consume them, yet they have found a stabilizing Rock on which to cling. This book is based on this amazing group of ladies, this sisterhood of overcomers, who have been the motivation and inspiration behind each word.

These ladies have allowed me intimate access to details of their lives and emotions that go much deeper than a typical doctor-patient relationship. I know when they are having marital problems or struggles with their kids. I am with them as they fight the hard battles of breast, ovarian, pancreatic, and colon cancer. I am by their side as they say their final farewells to their critically ill loved ones. I am involved with their emotional and spiritual healing through hardship and pain. I have the privilege of being able to witness their progression through the stressors and pressures of their lives. I get the unbelievable opportunity to watch them transform into jewels God can use to help others, and I call each of them priceless diamonds within the kingdom of God: the Diamond Society.

And they shall be mine, saith the LORD of hosts, in that day when I make up my jewels.

Malachi 3:17 KJV

God's Jewels

Does it seem as if you are only moments away from cracking up under the intensity of the changes surrounding you? Have there been days when you feel as if you are falling into a pit of uncertainty? Can you feel the rising temperatures heating the exposed surfaces of your life? Has your life been infused with pressure from every side? Does it seem as if you are being forced out of your comfort zone?

All God's jewels must be unearthed. There must be a time of deep concealment, as those issues that have threatened to bury you become the agents to develop greater clarity. Then there is a time of excavation, as God digs deep to find you at the core of your personal needs. Finally comes a time of exposure, when God showcases the adornments that have captured his heart. Through these times of intense pressure, heat, and upheaval, God reveals his diamonds.

Every facet of your life is a potential testimony. Every point of transparency is a place for you to reflect the light of his love. Even your imperfections are a part of your unique beauty. Every intricate detail is cut into your life for a specific purpose. Every variation in the colors of your journey are placed there by design. You are one of God's treasured jewels and a potential member of the Diamond Society.

Membership Criteria

You are already a diamond, a precious jewel of God. But to be a member of the Diamond Society you must meet the membership criteria.

1. You must love Jesus
2. You must love yourself
3. You must love others

As you embrace the concepts of the Free Woman's Creed, you will be well on your way to meeting the criteria. Membership is open to all who desire to be free. Free to love and free to laugh. Free to work and free to play. Free to give and free to receive. Free to hope and free to dream. Free to expect the impossible. Free to be free.

Eight-Week Group Study Guide

This study guide will help you share *Set Free to Live Free* in a group setting.

Week One

Chapter 1 Strange Medicine

1. What qualities in Cameron can you relate to?
2. What aspects of your life seem to be caught in a cycle?
3. In what areas do you feel you have lost control?
4. In what ways are lies you tell yourself mental ties?

Chapter 2 A Prescription for Living Free

1. Describe a time when it seemed as if Jesus had abandoned you.
2. What were you feeling during your perceived time of abandonment?
3. How would you describe your relationship with Jesus today?

4. Define in your own words: illumination, activation, transition, expulsion, and detachment.

5. Which stage of freedom do you believe has been your greatest obstacle?

Week Two

Chapter 3 *Perfection Is the Goal*

1. What does your "perfect life" look like?
2. How has this vision changed over the years?
3. Which statements in the illumination section describe you?
4. What is activating your desire to be free from perfectionism?
5. What can you do today to begin your transition to freedom?

Chapter 4 *I Am Perfectly Imperfect*

1. How do perfection and excellence differ?
2. What are your personal weaknesses?
3. How can these areas of weakness be an asset?
4. Which Scripture in the expulsion section encouraged you the most? Why?
5. How will cutting the ties of perfectionism affect your life?

Week Three

Chapter 5 *I Would Be Happy Too If I Had Her Life*

1. Describe a time when you were envious of someone's life. How did it make you feel?

2. What aspects of her life seemed "greener" than the grass on your side?

3. Which statements in the illumination section describe you?

4. What is activating your desire to be free from jealousy/envy?

5. What personal accomplishments can you celebrate today?

Chapter 6 I Am Too Unique for Comparisons

1. What have been some of the defining moments in your life?

2. What are the voices in the crowd telling you about yourself? Do you agree?

3. Do you view the Proverbs 31 woman as a role model? Why or why not?

4. Which Scripture in the expulsion section was most meaningful to you? Why?

5. How will cutting the ties of unhealthy comparisons affect your life?

Week Four

Chapter 7 If I Do This, I Can Look Like That

1. How has the media affected your opinion of your body?

2. Which statements in the illumination section describe you?

3. How would you describe your current diet and fitness plan?

4. Is your current plan beneficial or detrimental to your overall health? Why?

5. Answer the five questions in the transition section based on your current diet/fitness plan.

Chapter 8 My Body, My Temple, God's Choice

1. What types of foods do you enjoy? What is it about these foods that appeals to you?
2. Which activities did you enjoy as a teen/young adult? How can you modify these activities to make them a part of your life now?
3. Who has the final verdict on your physical appearance? Why?
4. Which Scripture in the expulsion section will be most beneficial as you embark on a healthier lifestyle?
5. How will cutting the ties of body envy affect your life?

Week Five

Chapter 9 Life Is an All-or-None Activity

1. What areas of your life have become a victim to the all-or-none way of thinking?
2. Which statements in the illumination section describe you?
3. What self-nurturing activities have you participated in this week?
4. What are ways you can incorporate small mental breaks within your day?
5. Plan an activity you will do this month just for pleasure.

Chapter 10 My Balanced Life Requires Addition and Subtraction

1. What season of life are you currently in? Describe what signs of this season you have been experiencing.
2. What does an aerial view of your garden look like? Which fields are in full bloom and which are lacking growth?

3. How would you define the quality of your life today? Why?
4. Which Scripture in the expulsion section was most meaningful to you?
5. How will cutting the ties of imbalance affect your life?

Week Six

Chapter 11 Being in Control Is Better Than Spontaneity

1. What areas of your life do you attempt to control?
2. How is control the enemy of freedom?
3. Which statements in the illumination section describe you?
4. What has control cost you?

Chapter 12 Spontaneity Is God's Opportunity to Surprise Me

1. Do you enjoy surprises? Why or why not?
2. What has been your experience with God's timing? How has it affected you?
3. Describe a time when you experienced a suddenly moment.
4. Which suddenly moment in the expulsion section would you like God to do in your life today?
5. How will cutting the ties of control affect your life?

Week Seven

Chapter 13 Emotional Imbalance Is Only for Crazy Women

1. Have you ever had an emotional attack? What events led to it?

2. Which statements in the illumination section describe you?

3. What is the condition of your foundation? Why?

4. How far have you allowed your relationship with God to go?

5. What is holding you back from seeking a more intimate relationship with God?

Chapter 14 My Transparency Opens the Door for Soul Connections

1. Name the people you are 100 percent transparent with, if any.

2. What qualities do these people possess that makes you trust them with the intimate details of your life?

3. What aspects of your life experience have you placed behind a veil? How can these experiences be used for God's glory?

4. Which Scripture in the expulsion section was most encouraging to you? Why?

5. How will cutting the tie of unstable emotions affect your life?

Week Eight

Chapter 15 Everything Comes with Conditions

1. Write your own list of life desires.

2. Do you believe God is able to make the things on your list a reality? Why or why not?

3. Which statements in the illumination section describe you?

4. What barriers to receiving do you have in your life?

5. How have these barriers affected you?

Chapter 16 *My Only Limitations Are the Ties I Allow to Bind Me*

1. What role do your mind and eyes play in freedom?
2. How do your eyes and arms help to put you in a position to embrace freedom?
3. What events in your past have contaminated your heart?
4. Which Scripture in the expulsion section was most beneficial in cleansing your heart? Why?
5. How will cutting the tie of self-imposed limitations affect your life?

Chapter 17 *The Diamond Society*

1. What mental ties are affecting your life? How?
2. What biblical promises can you use to break free from this mental tie?
3. What statements of the Free Woman's Creed are not currently a part of your life? How will you begin to incorporate them?
4. What "diamond" experiences have you had in your lifetime?
5. How have these experiences helped to form you into one of God's precious jewels?

Saundra Dalton-Smith, MD, is a board-certified internal medicine physician who has been practicing medicine since 1999. She treats a predominantly female population and has firsthand experience with the struggles women face trying to imitate the American dream. Dr. Dalton-Smith has been an adjunct faculty member at Baker College and Davenport University in Michigan. She lives in Alabama.